THE COUSINS PROJECT

FINDING LOST FAMILY AFTER THE HOLOCAUST

As Recollected by Descendants of the
Singer, Wites, and Torgovnick Families

Pamela Ruben

with Sandi Solomon, Geoffrey Bar-Lev,
Helen Singer-Katz, Monica Bialostocki Gutman,
and Sharon Fleitman

Elaine Person, Editor

CHB Media, Publisher

Copyright 2023 © Pamela Ruben and Others

All Rights Reserved
including the right of reproduction,
copying, or storage in any form
or means, including electronic,
in whole or part,
without prior written
permission of the author.

ISBN: 9798869137692

COVER PHOTOS CLOCKWISE FROM UPPER LEFT:

A LANDMARK CATHOLIC CHURCH IN ŁÒDZ
FAMILY RESIDENCE OM PIOTRKOWSKA STREET
THE I. L. PERETZ JEWISH SCHOOL IN ŁÒDZ
PALACE POZNANSKI IN ŁÒDZ (FRONT VIEW)

CHB MEDIA, PUBLISHER

(386) 690-9295
chbmedia@gmail.com

CONTENTS

Pamela Ruben's Prologue. 5
   Time Travel with Four Phone Numbers
Directory of Names 11
PART ONE: THE SEARCH
Chapter One: Discovering Lost Roots 13
Chapter Two: Digging Deeper. 15
   Discovering Geoffrey Bar-Lev And Helen Singer-Katz
   Discovering the Wites/Torgovnick Connection
Chapter Three: Sandra Torgovnick Solomon's Mission 21
PART TWO: STORIES FROM ŁÒDZ
Singer Family Tree Diagram 27
Chapter Four: Memories from the Cousins 28
   Geoffrey Bar-Lev, Memories of the Łòdz Ghetto
   A Holocaust Conference Changed Everything
Chapter Five: Geoffrey. 33
   Geoffrey Learns More about His Family
Chapter Six: Geoffrey Puts the Pieces Together. 35
Chapter Seven: Geoffrey's Parents.. 42
   More Questions Than Answers
   Surviving the Ghetto's Liquidation
Chapter Eight: Henry Survives a Death March 51
   Life in Communist Poland
   The Move to Israel
   Becoming Americans
   Visiting Poland
Chapter Nine: Helen Singer-Katz with Son, Daniel Katz. 70
   Family Spellings: Zyngier, Zinger, Singer
   A Return to Poland: Back to the Roots Trip
   A Land of Contradictions
   Remembering Edith (Edzia)
   New Perspectives on Family
   Viewing Henryk Ross Exhibit Brings Up Old Memories
   Jewish Identity

Chapter Ten: Monica Bialostocki Gutman. 90
   Family Surnames and Spellings: Wites, Perelstein
   Jewish Theater
   The Family Business
   The I. L. Peretz School
   A Legacy of Warped History
   Monica's Family

Chapter Eleven: Leaving Łòdz 104

Epilogue: Sandi Torgovnick Solomon. 106

PAMELA RUBEN'S PROLOGUE

TIME TRAVEL WITH FOUR PHONE NUMBERS

Sandra (Sandi) Solomon called me in May 2021 to tell me an extraordinary story of lost family connections, a story she wanted to share. "We have found four *undiscovered cousins* on our family tree, alive and well, seventy-five years after we thought that branch had perished in the Holocaust," Sandi informed me. She emphatically expressed her desire that their story be told and known. The cousins' parents (now deceased) were Holocaust survivors, most of them of the Łòdz Ghetto as well as extermination and forced-labor camps like Auschwitz and Buchenwald. These *new* cousins were born in Poland in the years shortly after World War II ended.

Sandi continued, "After my parents left Poland as teenagers (separately) in the 1920s with their parents and siblings, there is no record of contact with the family who stayed behind. After the war ended, there still was no news, so we assumed that none of the Polish family survived." Considering the large percentage of the Jewish population in Poland exterminated by the Nazis during the war, this seemed to be an unfortunate but likely conclusion. These *new* cousins, discovered through a dogged genealogy search in 2020, stemmed from both Sandi's maternal and paternal sides. They were all in their late sixties and early seventies, living in different parts of the United States. Sandi, already in her eighties, was eager to make up for lost time, to welcome these cousins into the family fold. With the pandemic raging, the first attempts to connect were made through Zoom meetings and phone calls.

While the new family members were for the most part happy to connect with their American-born cousins (Sandi and her immediate family), skepticism was a natural reaction at first. Sandi's son, Eric Solomon, shares, "So far, all relatives have been happy to meet us, though there is a bit of wariness upon initial contact, as you might imagine when a stranger reaches out claiming to be a long-lost relative. They are always surprised. Since September 2020, we have been establishing *new* relationships with *old* relatives (new to us).

After hearing the stories of her cousins' harrowing postwar childhoods in Poland, as well as their parents' traumatic experiences during the war, Sandi felt compelled to create a document to share with family and others who might have interest. "The fact that these cousins have come to light seventy-five years after the Holocaust is very, very unusual. They have gone through hell. I just feel their stories need to be told. I needed to become a messenger and stop the generations of silence."

As our conversation continued, Sandi asked me to consider writing the memoirs of her newly discovered family members. She suggested I begin my research by speaking with the family genealogist, Sharon Fleitman, Sandi's daughter-in-law (wife of son, Eric), had put in tireless hours reconnecting lost branches of the family tree and deserves credit for this long awaited and unexpected family reunion. Sandi also shared the contact information for her four new cousins, which I immediately uploaded to my phone.

I was intrigued by Sandi's request but expressed my reservations about creating a story centering around subjects I had never met in person, and given pandemic times and distance, possibly never would. Three of the four newly discovered family members chose to participate in what came to be known as *The Cousins Project*. I began to spend time getting to know the cousins through Zoom meetings, FaceTime, and on the phone. I heard their stories unfold and embarked on recording their memories from so long ago.

In my first phone call, I reached out to Cousin Geoffrey (Singer) Bar-Lev, who lives in Cumberland County, Tennessee and was born in 1948, just three years after the end of the war. From his first words, it was apparent that Geoffrey was both a charmer and a Nathanural storyteller. He quickly filled me in on his parents' background in the Lòdz Ghetto, where both parents were entrapped within its walls from the ghetto's opening in 1940 until its liquidation in 1944. Each lived separately with their own families, surviving on meager rations in small, airless quarters that housed up to ten families.

I searched the internet for photos of the ghetto for reference. Later, of course, I studied up on the history of Jewish Lòdz, and most specifically the ghetto, with Geoffrey becoming a valued instructor. Though he has been in the United States since the age of ten, Geoffrey has a distinctive but hard-to-place accent, reflecting his early years in Poland, Israel, and later Brooklyn. While technical difficulties (new phones, poor Wi-Fi, inputting of Zoom codes) interrupted our connections at times, Geoffrey rarely stumbled as he told his family history. When relating a particularly difficult story, he would break the tension by telling a joke or briefly shift from the scene and pull us back to the present. I remember chatting about Geoffrey's move from the Los Angeles area to rural Tennessee; he said his closest neighbor was a goat!

The first words of his family story took me on a journey to Lòdz's Freedom Square (Plac Wolnosci). His detailed recollection pulled me into a gray communist-looking plaza where he was strolling with his mother and baby sister, Helen on a mild spring day in the mid-1950s. While the weather was gentle, the antisemitic hooligans roughhousing in the park were not. I could feel young Geoffrey's discomfort as unwarranted slurs were tossed in their direction. While Geoffrey was too young to understand the meaning behind these insults, he comprehended that he and his family could not breathe or live freely in their homeland.

During our interviews, Geoffrey impressed me with his memory for detail, having left Poland at age eight. Despite his family's difficult past, Geoffrey was able to access youthful memories and recalled a wide range of emotions. While passing through Vienna by train on his way out of Poland, for instance, Geoffrey was struck by vivid colors he had not seen in his drab Communist homeland. He said, "It was hard to make sense of the fact that there was an alternate version of the dark and gray world in which we had lived."

After speaking with Geoffrey, I reached out to his younger sister, Helen Singer-Katz, in New Jersey. Born in 1952, Helen was just a toddler when the family left Poland. While she had limited memories of the family's life in Lòdz, she recounted a story of the mixed feelings she experienced after returning to Poland with her son, Daniel for his twenty-first birthday. She also shares what it means to be a second-generation Holocaust survivor, and how she has been impacted by her parents' trauma and collective memory.

My interview with Monica Bialostocki Gutman rounded out my conversations with the cousins. Monica is related to Sandi Solomon through her paternal side. On February 4, 2022, Monica reached out and called me. And I was so glad she did. Born in 1954, Monica was exceedingly open about her childhood and school years that took place in Lòdz, where she lived until her young adulthood.

Monica shared about her beloved *Jewish School* known as the I. L. Peretz School in Lòdz, a public school opened in 1948 that supported Jewish life and culture. Monica discussed her sheltered life as a *Peretznik*, growing up in a protected Jewish bubble supported by her parents Uszer Bialostocki and Fajgla Wites. A precocious reader, Monica held an adolescent/teen affection for Poland's romantic writers, and the work of one of her favorite writers played a fateful role in her family's eventual emigration. Censorship of his writings sparked protests that in turn led to new antisemitic persecution and the 1968 Uprising that caused many Polish Jews to leave the country. Monica's family left for Copenhagen in 1972.

As I spoke with the cousins, they reinforced one another's recollections about the harshness of growing up Jewish in postwar Poland. They each also shared bittersweet moments and introspection. Geoffrey noted that later in life he had heard there was a Jewish school in Łòdz and pondered if his early years in Poland might have been less fraught had he attended. Monica commented that the school was one of the few sanctuaries for Jews in postwar Łòdz.

The snippets each remembered about their early lives were surprisingly detailed: Monica remembered her black and white school uniforms with inserted collars. Geoffrey recalled having to hold his hands behind his back when his teachers addressed the classroom in the harsh public communist school system. At the same time, memory proved to be imperfect, as some of the anecdotes go back more than seventy years, and some were stories passed down (secondhand) from their parents. In other instances, there were minor discrepancies between family stories and documentation (sometimes dates were a bit off, other times it was the spelling of a name). When I pointed out these small differences, Geoffrey told me to "always go by what Sharon has found. She is the expert."

While the cousins hold strong memories from their own experiences, the recollections from their parents are more limited, especially of their time in the extermination camps and the ghetto. Memories and anecdotes of their horrific experiences were painful to recall and therefore sparingly shared by parents. Geoffrey muses that his parents tried to protect them with their silence about life in the ghetto, as well as the death camps. After experiencing so much loss during the Holocaust, many survivors like Henry Singer (Geoffrey and Helen's father) were eager to have families immediately following the war.

As I considered these memories, it became crystal clear that Sandi's new cousins indeed have a story that needed to be known. This story has no definitive start or finish, as it is a tale in progress with tragic beginnings and hopeful endings. This collage of memories is presented to pass on a story that almost wasn't. A story that was almost erased by the Nazi regime and their monstrous collaborators. A story that was so painful and complex to recount, it literally fell off the family tree.

Through their combined stories and collective memories, Sandi's cousins transformed a shady outline of the family tree into a colorful mosaic. While some stories have been unburied, gaps still remain. This story is told in the best of their memories, going back more than seventy-five years. Some names have been changed to protect privacy.

Please note that family surnames evolved through the years, through both imperfect record keeping (on Polish and Nazi documents) and later migration and assimilation.

DIRECTORY OF NAMES

Jerzy Zyngier—original Polish name
Jeff Singer—naturalized name
Geoffrey Bar-Lev—legally changed about 1992 when he started getting published on Jewish history. Current American name.

Halina Zyngier—original Polish name
Helen Singer-Katz—current American name

Golda Bialostocka or Bialostocki—original Jewish name
Gienia Bialostocka or Bialostocki—Polish name
Monica Gutman—American name

Sandra Torgovnick—original Polish name
Sandra Torgovnick Solomon and Sandi Solomon—current American names

PART ONE
THE SEARCH

Chapter One
Discovering Lost Roots

Sharon Fleitman has no formal detective training, but after doing a deep dive into her family's history, the amateur genealogist feels like one. "You have to be a little bit of a detective to push forward with your research. You need to have the interest and the desire to find the truth," she told the *Heritage Florida Jewish News*. "I decided to look into my family's history so my four kids would know (someday) about the people they came from."

The Washington University graduate and devoted mother of four young adult children had knowledge about her side of the family. "Over the years, I spoke with my mother-in-law, Sandi Solomon (née Torgovnick) about her side of the family tree." Sandi's parents, Jean (née Singer) Torgovnick (born in 1909 in Olesnica, Łòdzkie, Poland) and Nathan Torgovnick (born in 1909 in Stopnica, Swietokrzyskie, Poland), had come to the United States from Poland in 1923. Sandi was told that her grandparents' remaining siblings, as well as any descendants, perished in the Holocaust.

Sharon's husband, Eric Solomon, an Atlanta physiatrist, grew up believing all the Polish family had been lost. He said, "It was a done deal. I was told the family in Europe is lost, and there is nothing to say about it. My grandparents never brought it up. My mom's father, Nathan Torgovnick was from Poland. He didn't want to talk about any tragedy or lost family members. He came over as an adolescent with his parents and siblings, as did my maternal grandmother, Jean Singer. My great grandparents' remaining siblings stayed in Poland, and as far as we knew, all perished in the Holocaust leaving no living descendants. Most people are uncomfortable with loss but especially this generation. My grandfather would never talk about his life or family left behind in Poland. He would say, "I got on a ship to come here, and that was the beginning of my new story."

"There were no memorabilia from anybody in the past in my grandfather's house. He just had pictures of the immediate family—of my mom and her brothers. I guess he was forward looking."

Sharon and Eric wondered what had become of old family photos and letters. Sharon adds, "I don't know if they destroyed letters. (Were they painful reminders of loved ones left behind?) It was a very large family on both sides. I kept thinking, there's got to be letters or postcards. Were they lost or even thrown away? Where are the pictures? Where is anything?"

Sandi Solomon recalled a small stack of postcards that had been passed on to her from her father, Nathan Torgovnick. The dozen or so postcards written in Yiddish had been pre-war correspondence between her father and Polish relations. Nathan had shared that he sent money *home* monthly to his family members once he gained employment. Unfortunately, Sandi lost track of the postcards during her most recent move and regrets she had not translated them into English.

Chapter Two
Digging Deeper
Discovering Geoffrey Bar-Lev
And Helen Singer-Katz

While the family lacked documentation of their own, Sharon began to educate herself about available archives and resources. Additionally, she pushed her mother-in-law, Sandi Solomon, for more clues regarding her Polish family members. Sharon had uncovered that both sides of her mother-in-law's family came from the neighboring Polish towns of Stopnica, Olesnica, and Pacanów, which would become part of the search database. Sharon dubbed these three nearby towns as the *tri-city area*, with Stopnica the largest and the place where most records were kept and recorded. Sharon points out that some of the family later migrated to Łòdz. Sandi's father's connection with his hometown, Stopnica, became eternal when he and wife, Jean, were buried at the Stopnitzer section of Beth El Cemetery in Paramus, New Jersey, following their deaths in 1991 and 1997, respectively. (Stopnitzer refers to descendants of Stopnica, Poland.) Coincidentally, Henry Singer is also buried at Beth El Cemetery in Paramus.

Using the names of the towns as a geographical starting point as well as family surnames with names that had morphed over time, Sharon continued her pursuit. "Without a lot of trouble, I was able to find numerous helpful websites (Yad Vashem, Arolsen Archives from Germany, Jewish Historical Institute-Warsaw, and JRI-Poland). Getting detailed names and documentation was a whole other level of research."

Sharon viewed unburying the family like discovering the missing pieces of the family puzzle. "I began to reconstruct the family tree using documentation from those little towns not far from Łòdz, Poland."

Before World War II, Jewish cultural life thrived in Łòdz, which was the textile center of Poland. The Łòdz ghetto was the second largest of the Holocaust era after the Warsaw ghetto. From official registries, photos, and identification cards, Sharon learned that much family history seemed to have taken place behind the ghetto's walls. As she learned more about the inhabitants' dismal survival rate, Sharon began to prepare herself for the fact that Sandi's family members were most likely amongst the plus murdered by the Nazi regime. She held out hope that there might be unknown survivors 200,000 among them.

Sharon said, "I discovered the line of Henry Singer's family (first cousin to Sandi's mother, née Henryk Zyngier), through the Pages of Testimony archived at Yad Vashem, which he filled out in 1957." Sharon discovered last names that matched those on our family tree (Zyngier/Zinger/Singer). I started to reconstruct the line to see what became of them. Using this record, which contained a Tel Aviv address from Yad Vashem, I was able to match up Sandi's family name with the place, as well as the timing. It wasn't just the names that struck me about the Pages of Testimony, but the names coupled with the stated relationships. Zyngier/Zinger is a common surname; that alone would not have been enough to make the connection."

She continued, "Discovering these lost family members was amazing and terrible at the same time. There were documents showing that Henry had lost both a wife and a baby while imprisoned at Auschwitz. In addition to a photo of his late wife, I found a picture of Henry's work identification card while a prisoner in the Łòdz ghetto."

Despite family lore of total loss, Sharon had found a surviving family member. Later, Sharon would discover that Henry had passed away in 1969, coincidentally also buried at Beth El Cemetery in Paramus, New Jersey. Now that she had located a survivor, she wondered if there were any living descendants.

Sharon found her way to a Facebook group known as

the Jewish Genealogy Portal. "I posted one of the Pages of Testimony with the 1957 Tel Aviv address, asking members to help trace Henry on Israeli databases. One member with what he referred to as his *team* took up the cause. I don't know their methodologies, and they wouldn't reveal their sources, but in eight hours I was given the names of Henry's two living children as well as a contact. There were indeed survivors—Geoffrey Bar-Lev of Tennessee and his sister, Helen Singer-Katz of New Jersey!"

Sharon said, "After searching her name on the internet, I found Helen was a realtor. I located her email and sent a greeting along with some family information.

I didn't hear from her for a short while. Then, she private messaged me on Facebook and asked if I was the person that emailed her. I replied, yes, and we exchanged phone numbers.

Just like we had no clue we had living family members who had survived in Poland, Helen had no clue she had an unknown family in the US."

Sharon continued, "I am sure it was a lot for her to take in. I had all these documents (Sharon had been able to collect more than fifty pages of documents/images for her Ancestry.com family tree), but they were about her direct life. At this point, for me, it was more historical. But here she was, a living descendant pulled from pages of websites and lists. I had knowledge of the partially reconstructed family."

"What did I think of the lack of memorabilia between our families?" newly found cousin, Geoffrey Bar-Lev said. "Our side went through the Holocaust. In our household, there were only a handful of pictures left from the old days. But why did the family that came over have no memorabilia on their side? I can think of a few reasons. From what I understood about the Zeitgeist of the time, Sandi's grandmother came over just after World War I. They had to learn a new language, the mail was very slow, they had bad memories. The depression came on. Frankly, there were experts on this topic that say families lost interest in the ones they left behind. Maybe they felt guilty; I don't know. They had their own problems in their new country. Every group of immigrants that came to the US had their own problems with persecution."

Discovering the Wites/Torgovnick Connection

While searching through data from the United States Holocaust Memorial Museum in Washington, DC. Sharon uncovered a document from a court proceeding containing a name from the family tree: Wites. (Lipke Wites is the common descendant on the family tree. She is Sandi's grandmother and great aunt of Monica Gutman.) The artifact was written entirely in Polish, but Sharon ordered a copy through a contact she had made at the United States Holocaust Memorial Museum.

Sharon, the amateur researcher had built up connections through various genealogy groups and reached out through Facebook to a Polish language translator. "I belong to quite a few Facebook groups, and the Jewish Genealogy Portal came to my rescue once again. From my online conversations, I met a man named Ed who did a lot of translation from Polish and also teaches the language. I noticed his written English was particularly good. I contacted him through Facebook with an offer to pay. He refused compensation but offered to look at the document and to share a summary."

She continued, "I learned the document was a court record in which Fajgla/Fela Wites declared an uncle dead for the purposes of an inheritance. I am unsure of how that court filing turned out, but that mundane record was the decoding key. I was like, wait! There is another survivor!"

The translator suggested that Sharon write to the Jewish Historical Institute in Warsaw. (There's a museum and an archive there, and it was listed that Fajgla had been living in Lòdz.) Records from the Historical Institute revealed that Fajgla Wites had been living with her sister after the war. Sharon said to herself, "Hah! There are two more survivors." There was some additional information about Fajgla applying for entrance into the United States. "Apparently, they did not leave Poland, at least not at this point." Later, Sharon learned that the two sisters promised their father they would stay together, and one of them did not want to emigrate. Sharon said, "It blows my mind that any Jew would want to remain in Poland postwar."

Sharon reached out to her liaison at the Holocaust Museum. It turned out that this Wites line of the family did stay in Poland into the early 1970s. Then they left, emigrating to Denmark at that time. "I recovered another document requesting survivor reparations. We were able to uncover an address in Copenhagen from this document."

Sharon discovered an expat community of Jewish Poles who went to Copenhagen in the 1970s following the Polish government's anti-Zionist movement in 1968. After some additional legwork, Sharon was connected with Monica Bialostocki Gutman, who was now a resident of Columbus, Ohio!

Chapter Three
Sandra Torgovnick Solomon Discovers Her Mission

With her research completed, Sharon reached out to her mother-in-law and gave her the names and phone numbers of Helen Singer-Katz and Geoffrey Bar-Lev. While Sandi had a vague notion of Sharon's genealogy pursuits, she had no idea her daughter-in-law had found living descendants from her grandparents' family line.

Sandi recalled a time in the early 1970s when she received a cryptic phone call from her father to meet her at his home in Brooklyn. He said, "There are people here that I want you to meet." At that time, Sandi was a young wife and university student living in Bridgeport, Connecticut. She said, "My father had always been very silent about his past, and I had never received a summons like this. In those days, it was a big drive from Bridgeport to Brooklyn, but I went because my father rarely asked."

Sandi headed out to Brooklyn with her late husband, Steve. "We were introduced to my cousins from Toronto whom I had never met. There were four of them—two brothers and two sisters." Sandy learned they were survivors of the Holocaust, originally born in Poland with the surname Zeller/Zellowitz. (They were first cousins of her father on his paternal side—Torgovnick). That was the first Sandi had learned anything regarding her family and survivorship. "At that time, no one really said the word *Holocaust*. It did not appear (with frequency) in *The New York Times* or in the news."

When Steve took a position in Rochester, New York, Sandi and Steve visited her newfound cousins once a month or so. They last made contact about a dozen years ago. Sandi had been told *virtually nothing* about her European family in the years following the war. Sandi said, "The word *Holocaust* wasn't spoken (at least in my family) until twenty years after World War II was over. Also, I had never heard of the Łòdz Ghetto and was not familiar with the Jewish history of Łòdz until talking to Geoffrey over a period of months.

"I was disappointed by my own lack of knowledge about this place in history that had affected so many and taken members of my own family. I felt a mission to educate, to remember, and to bear witness for future generations. I wanted to share a personal picture as to what happened during the Holocaust based on a family story. Hopefully by stopping the silence (as Jews say), this will never happen again."

She continued, "It's such a personal story. It just hit me, and I think it will touch those who hear it: all this loss and hate makes no sense. The hatred that Hitler had for the Jews and the money and the time and the resources spent on hate. When I talk to my newfound cousins and see all the good they have done, I think there could have been six million more."

Sandi remembers contacting the first of the lost cousins, Geoffrey Bar-Lev. "We were both shocked to know that we did not know about one another. He didn't know anything about me, and I didn't know anything about him.

"We have been making up for lost time on Zoom. At my grandson's wedding in Atlanta two years ago, I met Helen Singer-Katz, her son, Dan, and her husband, Mike. I speak regularly with Monica Gutman on the phone and am looking forward to meeting her in person. Now I know these wonderful people, and it just boggles my mind about all those who were lost—not just for seventy-five years, but forever. I have made it my mission to welcome my undiscovered cousins.

Sandi Solomon's parents. Jean Singer Torgovnick and Nathan Torgovnick at Ohev Shalom Synagogue.

Sandi Solomon's maternal grandparents Anna Singer and Meyer Isaac Singer.

PART TWO
STORIES FROM ŁÒDZ

FAMILY NAMES DIRECTORY

Henry Singer (Naturalized 1964; née Henryk Zyngier; aka Hersh; other last name spelling found in documents: Zinger. 1914-1969

Geoffrey Bar-Lev (Naturalized 1964; née Jerzy Zyngier; aka Jeffrey/Geoffrey Singer) 1948-Living

Helen Singer-Katz (Naturalized 1964; née Halina Zyngier; aka Helen Singer) 1952-Living

Edith Singer (Naturalized 1964; née Edwarda Mysliborska; aka Edzia Singer; remarried, Edith Singer Milchman) 1916-2002

Singer Family Tree

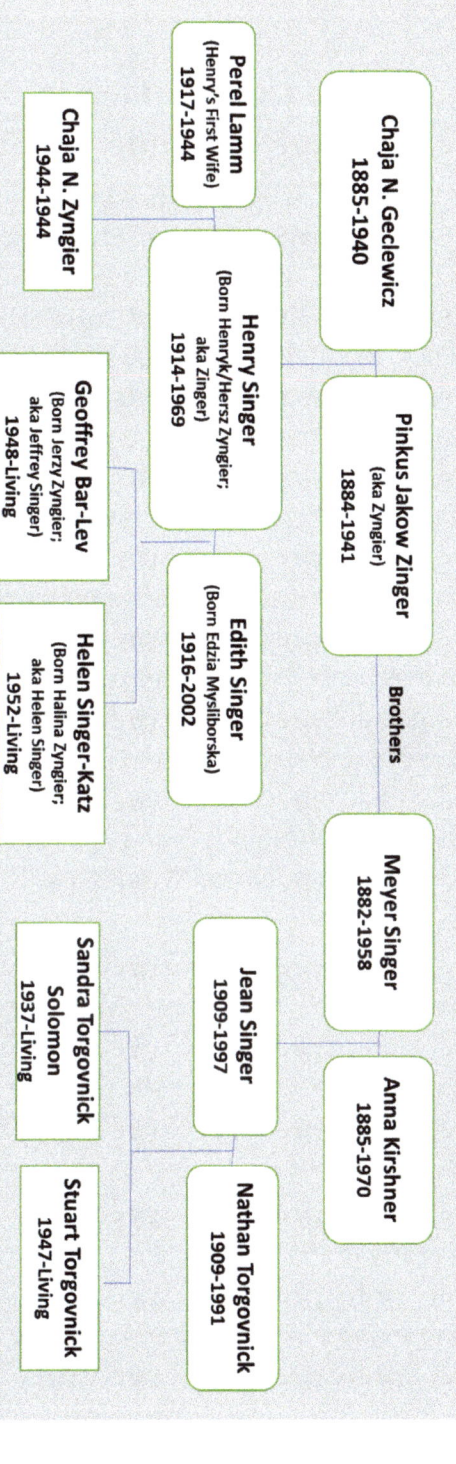

Pinkus Zinger and Meyer Singer were brothers. Meyer Singer was Sandra and Stuart's grandfather; Pinkus Zinger was Geoffrey and Helen's grandfather. Henry was a first cousin to Sandra and Stuart's mother, Jean. Henry and Jean's children, Sandra, Stuart, Geoffrey, and Helen, are second cousins. This chart is intended to clarify the relationships, and it ends on this genealogical line. It does not include children or grandchildren.

Chapter Four
Memories from the Cousins
Geoffrey Bar-Lev
Memories of the Łòdz Ghetto

"I would say we lived not far from what used to be the main entrance to the Łòdz Ghetto, the second largest ghetto in the Holocaust. And one of the ugliest places of its time," explained Geoffrey Singer Bar-Lev, a second-generation Holocaust survivor and adult child of two of the unlikely ghetto survivors. Though a boyish seventy-five, the retired publisher, Holocaust author, and businessman is anxious to share his collective memories, which weigh heavily on his conscience. His recollections overflow with the images of his late parents, who were burdened both with unspeakable loss as well as the uneasiness of survivorship while still both young adults. Additionally, his early years growing up in Poland in the late 1940s and early 1950s leave him with a taste of the antisemitism his parents and forebears endured. While Geoffrey has suffered from a speech impediment in the form of a mild to moderate stutter, he barely falters as he retells his family saga.

"When it got to be springtime in Poland and the sun would come out, we had nice warm days. My mother would take me walking in Independence Square because there was a statue in the middle with park benches all the way around. It wasn't exactly a square—more like a circle. If you Google images of Łòdz, Poland, you'll see it."

Geoffrey recalls the area as "very communist looking, and by that, I mean really drab and antiquated. Łòdz was very dreary up until the time we left, as if it lacked the technicolor of the free world." Geoffrey recalls that when he was a young boy, "they still had taxis that were horse and carriage."

On the *good days* (in the early 1950s, seven or eight years after armistice), their daily stroll was like a pastoral scene in a place you might live just about anywhere in the world, except, of course, for the ghosts of the ghetto in their midst where more than 200,000 Jews and others persecuted by the Nazis were worked, starved, or transported to their deaths. However, on most days it was clear the Singer family (Zyngier prior to 1964) were outsiders, as emboldened youths lobbed thoughtless antisemitic jeers, setting off unwarranted emotional minefields across their path. Out of nowhere they might hear, "Move over, Jewess. You're taking up too much room," as Geoffrey's mother did nothing more offensive than take her young son and baby daughter out to breathe the (not so fresh) air in post-war Poland.

"*Jewess, Jew*, and oftentimes worse. These words were foreign to me," comments Bar-Lev. "I couldn't comprehend why our neighbors hurled insults toward us and seemed to hate the fiber of our very being." At that time, Geoffrey was unaware of his own Jewishness, as well as the effects the Holocaust had left on his immediate family.

He said, "When I would ask my parents about what was happening around us (why the hate was palpable in the air), they always replied in hushed tones. Discussion of our past was almost unmentionable. I questioned if they were waiting for a safer time and place to let me in. It was not until we left for Israel, when I was eight, that I felt I could freely breathe and began to learn more about my Jewish heritage and who I was."

When Geoffrey's parents developed an awareness that their impressionable son was listening to these grown-up conversations, they began speaking of such things in Yiddish. "When they realized I could also understand Yiddish, they took their conversations underground. I imagined they wanted to spare our childhoods such thoughts."

Geoffrey continued, "Anyway, we *never* went to the other side of the former ghetto (which was the last remaining ghetto of the Holocaust until it was destroyed by the Nazis in 1944). And that didn't occur to me until many, many years later on my first return trip to Poland in 1999 when I put it all together. I realized what was going on and what was where. My mother avoided that entire area, and it was just known to be off limits."

The Holocaust and Geoffrey's deep connection to its tragedies didn't enter his consciousness until much later. Geoffrey said, "When we came to America, I wanted to become an American. Not just a Jewish American, I wanted to become *just* an American. I believed in America's ideals and that religion is one's private matter. In my pursuit of the red, white, and blue, I didn't think much about my background." He recalls struggling with foreign diction and the challenging sounds required in learning the English language. He stood in front of the mirror many times, placing his tongue *just so* as he practiced the *th* sound, unheard of in his native language.

After leaving for New York with his family in 1958 at the age of ten, Geoffrey put his interests in his familial history aside. "I knew what my family had been through, more or less. I paid attention to the conversations I overheard as I grew older—who went on what transport train and in what month. My ears perked up when I heard words like Auschwitz, Birkenau (part of the Auschwitz complex), and Flossenbürg—the camps where my father had been imprisoned and lost those most precious to him: his parents, his first wife, and the baby sister I would never meet.

"However, I did not think much about the reasons why mother avoided the main entrance of the former Lòdz Ghetto (where she had been imprisoned for five years) until I, myself, became a student of the Holocaust."

A Holocaust Conference Changed Everything

In 1987, Geoffrey's sister, Helen, traveled all the way from New Jersey to Los Angeles where he was living. Hoping to help her brother fill in some missing spaces in his life, Helen bought him a ticket to attend the Second Generation Holocaust Conference being held at UCLA.

The conference specifically targeted second-generation survivors like Geoffrey and Helen to help them process the inherited responsibility of bearing witness to their parents' memories. Geoffrey said, "It made me interested in my own history and where my parents came from. I was extremely interested in the Łòdz Ghetto, which stole (murdered) both family members and any sense of normalcy from my parents' remaining days.

"Prior to attending the conference, I just wanted to be *normal*, you might say." After attending his first conference, Geoffrey realized that he had an avoidance problem. "I began to understand why I was avoiding my parents' history, which was anything but *normal* and was also my shared history. It was discussed that second-generation survivors are victims as well. We grew up with parents who had suffered in unspeakable ways. How could that not affect us?"

After the meeting, Geoffrey worked with a therapist to get to the root of his avoidance issues. "I spent eleven and a half years in psychotherapy, and five of those years were almost totally about how the Holocaust impacted me through my parents, as well as the antisemitism that I lived through in Poland."

Geoffrey recalls a conversation with a college dorm mate in the 1960s. The friend stated the crux of Geoffrey's confusion regarding the antisemitic attacks of his youth (while still living in Poland). His college buddy stated, "You looked like them [other Poles]. You spoke like them. The only difference was your religious heritage (which was not visible to the eye). You must have thought something was wrong with you."

"My young friend hit the nail on the head," commented Geoffrey. "I felt like I was completely wrong. There was just something wrong with me. Growing up, I understood the difference between guilt and shame. Guilt is when you feel responsible about doing something wrong. Shame is when you are solely ashamed of your inner self, deeply embarrassed of everything. I felt guilty. My schoolmates in Łòdz made me feel like there was something wrong with me. I didn't understand what that thing could be. But I felt that way, anyway. There must have been something unnatural about me. My being wasn't acceptable."

In his search for self-acceptance, Geoffrey started reading everything that he could find about the Holocaust years, as well as antisemitism in Poland. Geoffrey immediately became fascinated in finding out what really happened—the underlying cause of all the shushing and secrecy during his childhood years in Poland. He began reading "everything in the English language" about the Holocaust. Then he became interested in a very personal story, the Łòdz Ghetto, less than a twenty-minute walk from his first home. The ghetto in which his mother, her sister, and his father, living separately, were among the small percentage of survivors, making the chances of his birth a statistical anomaly.

Geoffrey said, "Approximately at that time (the mid-1980s), a very thick chronicle came out about the Łòdz Ghetto from 1941 to 1944. I got very deep into reading about the Holocaust. In my own humble or not-so-humble opinion, I am a nonacademic expert on the subject. I studied the events of the Holocaust in various countries, as it wasn't the same in each country. Having lived there just after the war gives me a different perspective than most scholars."

After years of study, Geoffrey was inspired to share his knowledge of Jewish discrimination with American middle schoolers. In 1992, he co-authored *Discrimination: Jewish Americans Struggle for Equality*. He expresses his pride in reaching America's youth at an age of development when they "can still learn right from wrong." The book was widely distributed in American and Canadian middle schools and high schools.

Chapter Five
Geoffrey

Geoffrey Learns More about His Family

An energized Geoffrey returned from his first weekend meeting with his newly found cousins (March of 2021), Eric Solomon (Sandi's son) and Eric's wife, Sharon Fleitman. Prior to his weekend stay in their home in Atlanta, the group had met up in Chattanooga for a few hours—a middle ground between their homes.

As a twice-divorced, second-generation survivor, Geoffrey has limited familial connections outside of his sister, Helen Singer-Katz, her husband, Michael, and their son, Daniel. When Sharon reached out, he was excited about the possibility of growing his small family.

He gushed, "I just got back from my first weekend meeting with Sharon and Eric, which was absolutely wonderful. We went to all kinds of good restaurants, an art show, and a history museum."

"I was in the company of fantastic people. We have grown closer since we first met in person about four months ago. At that time, we met halfway between them and me. It was a good meeting but only a half day or so. First impressions? I feel a natural brotherhood with Eric, we have so much in common. And Sharon—I am so grateful that she found us."

As the family genealogist, Sharon offered Geoffrey an opportunity to look at the documentation she had uncovered. Geoffrey thought back to his first look at his family's wartime documents. Geoffrey said, "What impacted me most about looking over all those documents? God damn. It all impacted me the most. Suddenly 2021 was colliding with the 1940s. I was pulled back in time. I thought of my father's liberation.

We went over the family tree. I saw the documentation of my father's deportation. He was transferred to a concentration and labor camp called Flossenbürg after spending about two weeks at the death camp Auschwitz-Birkenau. I had never seen these documents before. I saw a picture of my father's first wife who went to Auschwitz-Birkenau [Birkenau is part of the Auschwitz complex. Geoffrey uses them interchangeably here] with him. They had a baby daughter who was four months old. That really shook me. I was aware that my father had been married before the war, though he didn't speak of it much. His wife's name was Perel. I believe the baby's name was Chaja. I'm not sure I have all the names right.

"My father had told me when they got to Birkenau, Perel was told if she gave up the baby, she might live. Like you would expect, she refused and was walked straight into the *showers*, with both mother and daughter perishing on their day of arrival. It was the end of August 1944. [A page of testimony filled out by Henryk Zyngier at Yad Vashem in 1957 reported that Perel Lamm died at Auschwitz in 1944 along with baby Chaja—whose name was misspelled as Chaim.] The SS was hurrying everything up. It was just before the US Army liberated that area. Everything was so tragic. Tragedy upon tragedy. He remarked upon the irony of baby Chaja's name deriving from the Hebrew root *chai* which means *life*.

"After about an hour and a half, I couldn't look at the array of pictures any longer. Sharon had located pictures of my grandparents. My father's family had a kosher bakery. His father was an Orthodox Jew with the beard and all the shtick that goes with it, which I could see in the picture."

Sharon Fleitman also reflected upon the heaviness of the documents she collected: "There were quite a few family members in that ghetto. Many Jews were drawn to Łòdz in the 1800s where they settled and set down roots because it was big in textiles and had jobs to offer." Initially, the names were just names on a list to Sharon. Once she began connecting with the lost cousins, her perspective shifted. Each name truly represented a person, an individual to whom she was related. Of all the documents collected, one hit Sharon hardest because it involved the loss of a child, a child linked to an infamous speech by Chaim Rumkowski. Rumkowski, leader of the Łòdz Ghetto is "not well-regarded in history," Sharon said. "He's thought of as a kind of traitor Jew who gave up his own peoIn December 1941, the Germans initiated the first evacuation from the ghetto. According to the Holocaust Encyclopedia, "The ghetto's Resettlement Commission, in consultation with Rumkowski drew up deportation lists that included unproductive ghetto residents, thousands of the recently arrived Central European and Polish Jewish families, and all the Roma inhabitants. Between January and May 1942, German authorities forcibly removed some 55,000 Jews, including nearly 15,000 children under age fourteen."

At the beginning of September 1942, Germans ordered another 20,000 people be deported. Then they demanded the sick, the elderly, and the children. Chaim Rumkowski communicated the order to ghetto residents in a September 4 speech including these horrifying words: "A grievous blow has struck the ghetto. They are asking us to give up the best we possess—the children and the elderly. I never imagined I would be forced to deliver this sacrifice to the altar with my own hands. In my old age, I must stretch out my hands and beg. Brothers and sisters: Hand them over to me! Fathers and mothers: Give me your children!"

Sharon explained further, "Rumkowski had to clear out the ghetto because they were bringing people from all over Europe. So old people and little kids (people who were not usable workers) had to go. But Rumkowski didn't say where they were going, and no one could imagine they would end up in a death camp.

"I found a document among our images, and the date on it corresponded directly to that speech. That one hit me." It was a deportation document for a ten-year-old boy named Josek Apolet, descended from cousins Basia Raja Torgovnick and

Eliasz Apolet. Josek was a second cousin to Sandi Solomon, just like Geoffrey Singer Bar-Lev and Monica Bialostocki Gutman. The deportation documents from Łòdz Ghetto show that the young boy was deported on September 12, 1942, to Chelmno Killing Center (Killing Centers preceded the more well-known concentration camps). His death is noted in the family archives as also taking place in September.

Sharon's sadness deepened when she discovered that Josek Apolet's entire line perished in the Holocaust. His name is included here so that it will be remembered.

Chapter Six
Geoffrey Puts the Pieces Together

"**Learning about the Łòdz Ghetto** from my family and from research, it was the ugliest scene in the Holocaust story. Well, one of the ugliest scenes. It was ugly because the appointed Jewish leader of the ghetto was told, 'You can handle the Jews of Łòdz, or we can do it for you.' So, he did it."

According to Geoffrey, "It was the Jewish administration running the ghetto, and they were the ones that put the names on the list to be transported out to camps. And Chaim Rumkowski, the leader appointed by the Nazi regime, governed the ghetto with an iron fist. He created a labor force that he believed would make the residents of the ghetto crucial workers and prolong (and potentially save) their lives. He had a Jewish police force, which he recruited from unsavory elements in Łòdz society."

Like many historians, Bar-Lev has pondered if the Rumkowski-led administration was a force of evil or a force of necessity. He comments, "If you interview people from the Łòdz Ghetto you get two opinions. One thought is that he was a collaborator. The other opinion is that he did what he could to save as many people as possible. And that is a legitimate argument, because he held the ghetto together for as long as possible, making its residents an essential labor force for the German effort." While the Łòdz Ghetto was the last ghetto to be liquidated (1944), according to the Yad Vashem website, the Germans viewed the ghetto as a temporary stay on the way to the Final Solution.

Geoffrey said, "All of this was done by Rumkowski and the administration of *Judenrat* [administrative councils made up of Jews compelled by Nazi Germany]. If you Google *Judenrat*, the SS did not give them that name. The name was used in the Middle Ages for the government created by Jewish communities."

Geoffrey's father, Henry became a resident of the ghetto

following his release from the Polish Army. "My father completed his compulsory service in the Polish Army in 1937. Henry was one of the very few Jewish noncommissioned officers." According to Geoffrey, Henry's commanding officers always liked his father. He was said to be a Jew even the SS liked. "When he was in Flossenbürg he walked in on the commander of the camp one time when he was having intercourse with his mistress. The mistress took her lover's pistol and was going to shoot my father. 'Shoot him, shoot him,' she cried. The Nazi officer wouldn't shoot my father. Most likely because he was a very charming person.

"My father was recalled into the military the summer of 1939, when the Germans were claiming that the Polish troops entered German territory. They made up this excuse to invade Poland. In the background there were negotiations between the Germans and Russians who had made a pact to divide Poland in half—half to Germany and half to the Soviet Union. Łòdz was incorporated into greater Germany."

After a stint as a POW in Czechoslovakia, Zyngier was released to Łòdz just as the ghetto was established (opening in February 1940 and sealing its gates later that spring. Its residents were imprisoned behind a wooden and barbed wire fence with many sentry points). Though a veteran of the Polish Army, Henry was a Jew first to the Nazi regime. His previous service and likability were irrelevant, and he was imprisoned along with the first 100,000 plus Jewish residents. Geoffrey comments that at the ghetto's height there were 260,000 entrapped within its walls.

Geoffrey said, "Every able-bodied person in the ghetto worked. Those who did not work were in danger of being transported out of the ghetto." With his military background, Henry was assigned a job to guard the food supply outside a giant warehouse. Food in the Łòdz Ghetto was scarce. A large percentage of the ghetto's residents died from starvation as well as exposure to the elements. Geoffrey explained that as a guard, his father was fed better than most. "Not so much because he had access to the food supply but because his role as a guard required him to have strength." Geoffrey adds, "He was handpicked by the ghetto administration for this position because in the military he had a *rep* for being honest and trustworthy. He wasn't the only guard. The food was guarded around the clock in shifts."

Henry pocketed leftover food to share with his first wife, Perel. "The reason why my father's first wife was able to get pregnant in the ghetto was because she was getting extra food and nutrition. Many women were not able to conceive because of the near starvation conditions.

"The most striking thing my dad told me about daily life in the ghetto was the fear of the Jewish police force, which was instructed to shoot escapees on sight. He told me that Rumkowski created the police force to enforce what the Germans wanted. These were the guys who had the names and addresses of the people who were to be transported. Anyone who was sick, anyone without a job in the ghetto, anyone who did not get along with their boss in the ghetto, anyone who was a problem of any kind was put on that list. And they were told to show up at a train station right next to the ghetto and told to bring no more than ten kilos of belongings with them.

"They didn't know where they were being sent, but rumors began to float around that Auschwitz (a likely destination) was a bad place. I don't think they were able to comprehend what was happening. I imagine residents wondering, 'How can they kill us if they need us for the war effort?' There was no precedent for it. They couldn't believe it. Human beings and human nature are that we should not comprehend our own death."

Henry remained in the ghetto until its liquidation which began between June and July of 1944, with the last train out of Łòdz in August of that year. Geoffrey believed his father had to have been on one of the last transports.

Henry, Perel, and their four-month-old baby, Chaja (Chaya) were sent to Auschwitz-Birkenau. "Once there, they took you off the train and the men were separated from the woman as part of the selection process. Then the able-bodied (potential) workers were separated from the elderly and those unfit to work. This meant if you were told to go left, you would see these brick buildings that looked permanent. However, they were for the most unfortunate who were sent to the gas chambers.

"In this particular case, with the Russian army on the Germans' heels, if you didn't make it into selection, you went right into the gas chambers. There was no time left; the end of the war was closing in. They weren't even tattooing prisoners anymore. Anybody that was strong or had any kind of a usable trade was transported to concentration camps for slave labor for the German effort."

At right is the Grand Hotel in Łòdz as pictured in the 1940s and 1950s. Below is the Łòdz Ghetto as seen during Nazi occupation in WWII.

Chapter Seven
Geoffrey's Parents
More Questions Than Answers

Geoffrey said, "**According to old records**, my mother was born in Lòdz, Poland in 1916, and was named Edzia Mysliborska. Poland had been partitioned for the past century, at times by Russia, Germany, and the Austro-Hungarian Empire. Poland wasn't its own country once again until after World War I." Before World War I, Lòdz was governed by Germany, Auschwitz was governed by the Austro-Hungarian Empire, and the eastern area was governed by Russia.

"After World War I, my mother had to re-register and take on a Polish name. Her new Polish first name was Edwarda. The Polish *W* is like a *V* sound. I called her Mama, but everyone else still called her Edzia (*dz* is very close to the *J* sound in English). Her name in America later became Edith. Mama claimed she was born in 1918, but we had seen prior documentation that she was born in 1916. We always used to tease her, 'Mom, when were you really born?' [Her Lòdz birth records specified her birth year as 1916.]

"My mother was from an educated and upper middle class family. Lòdz was the third largest city in Poland, and it tried to keep up with Warsaw and Krakow in terms of cultural offerings. Mama had attended a gymnasium, which is like an American high school that prepares you to be university bound. In contrast, my father only had a fifth-grade education because his family was poor. This meant there was no choice but to send him to work. Despite Lòdz being a rough place to grow up post-war, my mother was determined to refine me, exposing me to the arts."

"She was interested in education and wanted me to know and experience things. We had this painting in the living room depicting Napoleon escaping in the winter from Russia. I was entranced by that magnificent work of art. As a young artist, I attempted to copy it many times. I looked at it, trying to remember lines, angles, as well as overall imagery. Then, I would do my best to draw horses driving in the snow. That was all her influence: arts, music, education. She was always urging me to improve my manners and to act like a little gentleman. I can still hear her daily reminders, 'You don't do *this* in front of other people. You don't do *this;* you don't do *that*.'

"She made sure that I ate like a European. She was fastidious about that. I had to eat with a knife and fork in the Continental or European style. When cutting the food on our plates, we did not switch hands and swap the knife and the fork like we do in the US. When I first got here and saw Americans stab their piece of meat with a fork like that, I lost my appetite."

Edith took little Geoffrey to the opera and the ballet. She encouraged him to sketch and draw, which he often did. "By the age of six, I could play the piano." Geoffrey recalls his strict music teacher offering "more stick than carrot." More than sixty years later, the former piano student can still picture his instructor lifting him up by the collar of his shirt, grabbing him harshly by the ears. "I had to practice my chords all the time."

While Edith was eager to share cultural experiences from her childhood, she remained closed about her life during the war. "Getting my mom to talk about life in the ghetto was like pulling teeth, the same for my father. Mama was a young adult during her imprisonment. I asked questions as I was growing up. It was hard to know which questions to ask and the ones that might be answered. So, I chose very simple questions as I was still a child and then a teenager. In the early '60s, my curiosity shifted to the hippie movement and what was happening in America. It's all a bit of a smoky haze."

When Geoffrey was younger, he would take walks in the evening and talk about "all kinds of things" with his father. Geoffrey's father, Henry was born in 1914 and died in 1969.

After the war, Henry Singer was no longer the affable soldier who had charmed his superiors. Years of loss and suffering had turned his emotions inward. On these walks, Henry wasn't quiet or reserved. Instead, Geoffrey recalls his father as angry and fuming. "He was always fuming. He was hooked on war movies where the Germans were clobbered, and the Americans and the Brits won. My father watched those movies, and to some extent he put himself into the movie, vicariously feeling the win."

As a young boy, Geoffrey wanted to be a soldier, someone his father would openly admire. "I would put my hands over my head and find small holes on the side of a building. Then, I would ask my father, 'What is this?' He would walk around pointing out bullet holes left over from the war."

While Geoffrey and his father spent time together watching war movies. (The 1967 World War II movie *Tobruk* comes to mind. Geoffrey describes it as the kind of movie his father was *hooked on* with montages of the British defeating the Germans.) The young man could feel space between himself and his father; the war had stolen his affability and charm. "There was a rage growing inside him, like cancer. I felt his inability to get close to me. He never attended my soccer games, which was a sport played by all the local kids. He never took me anywhere." Geoffrey couldn't help but notice the faded remnants of whip marks that scarred his father's back and the screams from the nightmares that awoke the household.

"Both my parents wasted away their young adulthood in the ghetto, but separately. My father didn't talk much about his first wife. Even if he hadn't been married, chances are he would never have met my mother in the ghetto. It was so damned crowded, they had installed three pedestrian overhead bridges, which you see in all the pictures. Traffic cops ruled over the massive pedestrian population. It was that crowded." Geoffrey's parents never met until after the war.

After the war Geoffrey's mother and her sister opened a hat business, becoming milliners. With practically no funding, the two enterprising women took over a storefront, and started making hats. "They had absolutely no money after the war. I imagine there was a minimal start-up fee and an unlimited desire to succeed. My parents met one another through the business. My father needed a job, and they hired him. I can imagine the sisters thinking, *Somehow, we are still alive and making hats.*

"Studying and thinking about my parents' experience in the ghetto has left me with more questions than answers. I have spoken more of the ghetto than my mother ever did. My mother remains a mystery until this day." Geoffrey does know that a twenty-four-year-old Edith was sent to the ghetto with her younger sister, Dorka (who later became known as Doris when she found refuge in Canada). The sisters shared housing with their strict and protective father, Abram Jakub Mysliborski. [It is noted on Edzia's birth record that her father and mother are unmarried at her birth. They married in 1922.] With eight to ten people jammed into one-room apartments, it's certainly possible they were smashed in with other families, as well.

Geoffrey recalls that the grandfather he never met because of tragic time and circumstance was referred to as Yaakov—a Jewish name for Jakub. Edith's mother, Perla (née Kochanska) Mysliborska, had died of cancer in 1938. Geoffrey can't help but wonder if her premature death spared his maternal grandmother from other kinds of suffering.

"In February of 1940, my mother along with more than 100,000 other Jews and innocents were pretty much ordered to move into the most decrepit neighborhood of Łòdz (Baluty). They were slowly imprisoned in this four-square-mile area of squalor. Calling it a neighborhood would be generous. There was no sewer, electricity, or running water. Imagine being told to move from your home to your town's worst neighborhood—or else." With no sewer system, the ghetto was very secure (other Nazi-enforced ghettos used open sewer lines as a means of transporting goods and people), and it made the smuggling of food and medicine incredibly difficult."

"Within a three-month period, nearly impenetrable walls were erected around the thousands of people, including my mother, imprisoned within. Barbed wire, walls, and fences were in place by May 1, with the ghetto *closing* on April 30."

"May Day, which as you know is May 1, was always a hard day for the Jews in Poland, as well as other notable days (both Jewish and secular). The Nazis traced May Day, a celebration of workers' rights, to Karl Marx—a renowned Jew. They had an *interesting* history of causing the Jews pain on all types of celebratory days. And May Day in the Łòdz Ghetto was no exception."

"The ghetto made life unbearable on so many levels. There was a horrible lice problem. It became impossible for people to sleep in their apartments. Nobody wanted to talk about ugly things like this. People were wearing rags and didn't have access to showers. I am unable to describe the filth and horror in which they lived."

As a youngster, Geoffrey was curious about his mother's life in the ghetto but didn't always know the right questions to ask. "I had always wanted to know if she had a boyfriend before she met my father. It seemed like such an awful place to go through alone." When Geoffrey was a teenager, Edith revealed that she indeed had a boyfriend during those years. "Did he survive?" was the first question from a surprised young Geoffrey. The high death rate in the ghetto made his survival highly unlikely. "He lived," his mom responded. She had followed his journey from afar, discovering he had made it safely to Minneapolis.

"From what I remember my mother was a seamstress in the ghetto, with everyone exploited by the Germans working for their lives. Prior to the war, Łòdz was a top textile maker for Poland. They were slave laborers. She could have made a variety of things the Germans needed for the war effort from belts to troop attire, backpacks, knapsacks, even clothing that was sent to German boutiques and department stores.

"I always wondered if she met her boyfriend in stolen

moments at the factory. Old, historical photos show packed rooms of seamstresses and tailors lined up with endless rows of sewing machines–sweatshop style. Could they have worked on the same line?"

"One of the few things Edith did mention was the intense level of hunger. She would say, 'We were so hungry, if we had anything to eat, we would lick the crumbs off the table, and lick our empty fingers and savor the memory of the taste.'"

The late fall of 1940 was an especially difficult time. Geoffrey's grandfather became deathly ill. While Geoffrey does not know his grandfather's particular ailment, typhus was rampant and took the lives of many. Though medications were scarce, Geoffrey shares, "There was always a little smuggled in. You had to know the right people." He referred to connecting to the right people as "Polish protection"—having an *in* with someone in the administration.

"If you knew someone in a position of power, maybe you could help a cousin whose name was put on the wrong list or possibly procure some medicine for a sick relative. I always wondered, *Who did you have to know (and what did you have to do in return) to pull off this shi*"Throughout history when people are in dire situations, there has always been a form of negotiation. I always wondered if my mother and her sister were preyed upon as two attractive single women. What did they have to do to get their father medicine as well as survive?

"I thought, perhaps, those were some of the reasons my mother was terrified by (the location of) the ghetto's former gates. She must have been haunted by memories of their desperate circumstances, as well as the things one had to do to survive. In my mother's particular case, she was locked behind the ghetto walls for almost five years, from the opening of the ghetto to its liquidation.

"I have always had so many questions for my mom and my aunt. They were very secretive about their time in the ghetto. I can understand they were extremely vulnerable. Today, we are so conscious of hate crimes. I feel women are one group who are still singled out."

Edzia and Dorka were at their father's deathbed when he passed. Records show that he died on November 11, 1940, surviving in the ghetto for less than nine months. With grave concern for his daughters' survival, Yaakov passed on some last thoughts including, "If you stay together, you will survive."

Surviving the Ghetto's Liquidation

The sisters heeded their father's advice. They protected one another as if their very survival depended on it. And it did. When the ghetto was liquidated, and in the case of the Łòdz Ghetto, emptied of evidence of its countless crimes against humanity, the pair managed to stay together. Most of the remaining residents (70,000 were still there in the summer of 1944) were sent to Auschwitz or other death camps, including Geoffrey's father, first wife, and baby daughter. Dorka was amongst the 900 or so inhabitants chosen to stay behind by a ghetto official.

Bravely, Dorka asked if her sister, Edith could stay, too. A simple question like, "Can my sister stay, too?" could be life-threatening. Commanding officers were known to shoot ghetto prisoners for much lesser offenses.

Geoffrey explains, "There were close to 900 (877) surviving residents in the ghetto itself when the Soviets entered the ghetto, and 700 had been chosen at random, including my mother and her sister, to stay in the ghetto after everyone was deported. Their instructions were to go through the apartments and salvage anything that might be useful for the Germans. The Germans knew they were losing the war and were determined to get everything of value, including items left behind. While the sisters' lives had been spared, they were faced with the unsavory and horrifying job of picking through the items abandoned by those who had been sent onto the trains.

"An additional 187 people did not go on the trains but went

into hiding. Because the Germans were losing the war on the Eastern front, they didn't have the manpower to go after people hiding within the ghetto. The ghetto was surrounded by 213 sentry points, so it was a prison itself."

Geoffrey describes the sisters as inseparable thereafter. "When Dorka left for refuge in Canada in 1952, my mother wanted to leave as well." However, his father, Henry, wanted to stay. Not only was Edith pregnant with their second child, but things finally seemed to be coming together for him. "Money was flowing from the business like it never had before. He was able to buy the finest clothes, furs, and jewels for my mother. Also, my father was very Polish. It was said that even the antisemitic Poles liked him. This disagreement about emigrating may have been the beginning of a longtime resentment between my parents.

At left is Piotrkowska Street in Łòdz as it looks today. Above is Freedom Square in Łòdz. Seen below is the rear entrance to Palace Poznanski in Łòdz.

Chapter Eight
Henry Survives a Death March

"**My father had three brothers** at the beginning of the war. The oldest, Majer, was caught smuggling food into the ghetto. He was either executed right away or sent to his death in Chelmno. No one knows what happened to his other brothers, Lazer and Levy as well as his sister Sheindel. According to records collected by Sharon, Majer was a young father when he entered the ghetto. His entire family line was lost, including his wife, Rosa, and two young sons, Shlomo Yosef and Burech, who was known as Benik. Both boys died before the age of ten."

Life was also harrowing for those who managed to survive. "Near the end of the war, my father had been transferred to Flossenbürg (labor and death camp). The SS put the remaining Jews on a death march (a forced camp evacuation at the end of the war. Unfortunately, there were death marches from many camps as the Nazis tried to remove evidence of their existence) that lasted almost thirty days," according to Geoffrey. In the final days only about three thousand remained alive, including Geoffrey's father. Henry was marched from Flossenbürg camp between Nuremberg and the Czechoslovakian border. (The dates were most likely September 19 until sometime in April).

"When they got to the outskirts of Lidice, Czechoslovakia, the commanding SS officer abandoned all these emaciated Jews. The war was almost over, and they were worried about repercussions and war crimes—that they might be held accountable by the allies. He decided to leave them there and split."

Eventually the Red Army found the emaciated group of survivors. "Since it was obvious the survivors were starving, they started giving them food," Geoffrey noted. "These were real country boys from the Russki countryside, not sophisticated in the care of emaciated war refugees. Because my father had military training and had been a POW, he knew not to eat the food after so many months of starvation, that his body would not tolerate the sudden intake of calories. Even though my father only had an elementary school education, he had an education from life in the military." Later, Henry would learn that survivors who were fed any solid food following starvation suffered deathly consequences.

Life in Communist Poland

"You might imagine that World War II ended in 1945 or 1946 when armistices and proclamations were signed. While life may have transitioned back to normal in the US, life in Poland would never know that kind of normal. Communist regulations were present everywhere." Geoffrey can remember political cartoons of the American President Eisenhower with atom bombs jutting out from all his pockets. Schools became conduits of communism and were bound by harsh rules. He remembers shiny varnished floors and changing from outside shoes to inside slippers at school. The uniform was coarse, and he recalls feeling restrained in the elbow and the forearm. "It was especially awkward when we got into the classroom and were required to sit straight up with our hands behind our backs.

"'Liced Jew.' That's what I was called as the only Jewish student in my Lòdz public school where I attended until the second grade. Recently, I heard there was a Jewish school in the area, but at that time I knew nothing about it. Perhaps if I had attended, I would have been more accepted, less bullied. During my early school days, I felt there was something wrong with me by the way they laughed at me and picked on me, attacking me after school."

As a spirited kid, there was a time when Geoffrey tried to fight back and throw a punch or two at his aggressors. But the odds were not in his favor. "Soon, it became three and four kids against one. So, I began to run away. Stupid I was not."

Wise beyond his years, the elementary schooler protected his parents by not burdening them with this "nasty business" at school. He could see it pained them to watch their eldest child relive the antisemitism of their youth. "I was the only Jew. I didn't have any real friends. I didn't know any other Jewish kids."

Although life in newly communist Poland was rough, not everything was bad, especially at first. In the early 1950s, the Singers lived in an expansive apartment in a nice neighborhood on Próchnika Street. His beloved Nanny Stefcia was like a second mother to him. He remembers her as a warm and nurturing person. Food was plentiful, cooked and served in a very old-world style. Geoffrey recalls his father returning from trips to the market with squawking live chickens. Stefcia processed (slaughtering and cleaning) them at the sink. He also remembers his nanny spending time with his little sister, Helen. She was very protective of both children.

Geoffrey recollects a Persian rug under a large dining room table that covered almost the whole dining room floor. He remembers tying silver tablespoons to his socks, as he pretended to skate across the hand-laid flooring.

During the summers, the family enjoyed an extended vacation at the Baltic Sea as well as wintertime Christmas vacations in Zakopane (Poland's most famous winter resort). His aunt's family, who had found refuge in Canada, sent toys that "nobody else had." Geoffrey's parents encouraged him not to talk about his shiny playthings, as they were not looking for additional ways to set him apart.

While the natives were not friendly, Geoffrey did have one special pal. "Christina was my first love in the first grade. She would sit with her back against the wall, and I would wedge myself beside her. We had a crush—I liked her, and she liked me." However, Christina's Catholic neighbors were not tolerant. When Geoffrey bicycled to her neighborhood after school, it was not uncommon to be met with a hailstorm of rocks. Moving quickly on his bike, Geoffrey did not hesitate to throw rocks right back. "I had my bicycle, and I had good aim." He reflects, "Later, all the practice I had throwing made me a better pitcher and athlete."

Though there was some satisfaction in being able to fight back (unlike when he faced an angry gang at school), he would return from these visits saddened and confused. He would ask his mother why people hated him (what does it mean to be Jewish?). She said, "They are stupid. Don't listen to them."

Despite his father's financial success as a middleman in the wool business, Geoffrey's family lived in an atmosphere of perpetual fear. With the communists slowly gaining control, he recalls his parents often putting their fingers to their lips, shushing him with frequency. He was reminded not to talk about his toys or pretty much anything that could call attention to his family.

When Geoffrey's parents wanted to ascertain "what was really happening in the outside world," they would listen to Radio Free Europe, which was banned by the communist world for its free expression, which included "real news and the truth." There was so much concern about discovery, that windows were covered while listening, with both the radio and his parents positioned underneath a blanket.

Sometime in 1954, there was a midnight raid on Geoffrey's house as well as the home of his father's business partner. (Geoffrey can remember being awakened in the wee hours of a Sunday morning but cannot place the time of year.) The Secret Polish police found a stash of US dollars. Geoffrey's father and his partner were dragged away separately to prison. The sleepy six-year-old felt deep confusion; his mother stayed "mostly silent."

Geoffrey explains that under communist rule, every enterprise had a quota for earnings. His father's company was reported for making too much money, exceeding the quota for production as well as income. After nine months of imprisonment, Henry was released. Geoffrey shares that his father bailed out his partner before himself. "His partner, Israel, had a wife and three children.

When Israel's wife found out he was going to be in jail for five years, she went to the roof of their apartment building and jumped off, taking her life. There wasn't anyone to care for the kids, so my father told my mother to use our money to get Israel out of jail. Then she had to use the rest of our money to get my father out of jail. How this was done, I don't know exactly. I think some former officers in the Polish army who liked my father were able to pull strings, but pulling strings costs money. We ended up very poor by the time we got to Israel.

"My mother would put my sister in a carriage and take us out for walks past a government building that must have served as a prison. We would see a man in the window on the third or second floor. My mother would point toward the man and say, 'That's your father. Give him a wave.'" After Henry's release, Geoffrey's parents began planning to leave for Israel.

The Move to Israel

Geoffrey said, "I wasn't told much about our move to Israel." One fall day in 1956, Geoffrey's parents told him that the family was leaving Poland and moving across the world. "I was eight years old and not part of any decision-making process, as you might imagine. I recall some guys coming to our house and putting our personal effects into huge crates. Sometime after that (which may have been the next few days), my parents woke me and Helen up at about 3:30 a.m." The family was taken by car to Warsaw, about an hour and a half away (about 136 KM or 85 miles).

Geoffrey remembers riding in an old Citroën automobile and staying overnight in a Warsaw hotel. In the morning, the family boarded a train to Bratislava, at that time in Czechoslovakia (now the Czech Republic and now the capital of Slovakia). At the border, troops boarded and inspected the train. It was unclear to Geoffrey whether the Secret Police were Czechoslovakian or Russian. Either way, they were an intimidating reminder of life under communist rule. Geoffrey remembers, "They were all clad the same way, and each soldier was armed with (what appeared to be) an AK47. They stood in military formation about ten meters apart. To me, they looked like Gestapo guys from the movies wearing long leather coats." The secret police marched from compartment to compartment, checking for papers and searching through luggage.

"We did not travel first class. By the time we were leaving Poland, we were destitute. Our closed compartment looked like the kind in the movie To Russia with Love—seats on each side with bunks above. My father and I always slept up high. Helen and my mother slept below."

When one of the policemen entered the Singer family sleeping compartment, he snapped, "Papers, please," in the direction of Henry and Edith. Henry handed the soldier his exit visa papers. The Singers understood that the word "please" was merely a formality. It would have been more appropriate for their intimidator to command, "Papers, or else!" Geoffrey could feel the nervous energy emanating from his parents as the soldier barked, "Are these your children? Is this your luggage?" His father said yes to the questions. Nevertheless, the contents of the luggage were tossed and searched.

Finally, the inspecting policeman turned on his heels to leave. But, alas, there were some final questions. Henry was asked briskly, "Why do you want to leave the communist world? Don't you like living in the communist world?" In Geoffrey's mind, the troops had demonstrated many of the reasons the family was fleeing Poland. Though only eight years old, he was shaken and angered by the soldier's demonstration of complete authority. Geoffrey had no doubt that his father felt much the same way.

Fortunately, Geoffrey's father did not have the impetuousness of a young child. As a veteran soldier and former prisoner of war, Henry Singer knew just the right tone for speaking to the soldiers. Speaking deferentially and as affably as was appropriate, Henry briefly stated, "We are Jews, and we want to go to Israel." Geoffrey remembers the soldiers lingering for a moment as his father's words hung in the air. The answer must have been an acceptable one, so they made their way out of the family's compartment.

Geoffrey recollects, "It's hard to say how much time the searches took. The soldiers tossed through the entire train. Suddenly, the train surged forward with its first chug. Soon, it was chugging away. We were moving. I looked at my mother's face, and the relief in her eyes I couldn't even begin to mimic.

"All of a sudden, we arrived in Vienna, my first Western country and the next leg in our long journey to Israel. My mind was blown by all the lights and the endless variety of stores, which had their doors flung wide open." The fanciful merchandise and friendly proprietors seemed to beckon customers into their vestibules. "My jaw dropped as I took in all the different kinds of goods in vibrant colors that people could buy. In Poland there were no neon or bright lights like these. People dressed in all the same drab colors: navy blue, black, gray."

Geoffrey couldn't help but notice the crowds of people who were walking around bright-eyed and merry. "We have left behind the sad and grim faces of my homeland," Geoffrey thought to himself, "I have magically found myself in a part of the world where there is happiness and joy in people." It was hard to make sense of the fact that there was an alternate version of the dark and gray world in which he had lived.

As they disembarked the train, Geoffrey was curious to try things available in this new place. "I don't know where this thought came from, but I really wanted to eat a banana. There were no bananas in Poland. I had never seen a banana, but for some reason I knew that you shouldn't eat the peel." My mother bought me a banana and showed me how to eat it. Henry gobbled up his banana and was "as sick as a dog." Nevertheless, he had a taste for exploring this new world.

The family stay in Vienna was all too brief, as it was just a stopover for the flight to Athens the next morning. "We were in winter clothing because in Poland it was late fall. Athens was hot as hell, and I remember taking off everything that I could. We changed airplanes and landed in what is now Ben Gurion airport in Tel Aviv."

Tel Aviv throbbed with construction projects. The new buildings were all white, mostly fabricated of Jerusalem stone. "Poland wasn't white. Everything there was gray, old, and dreary, especially Łòdz. It was a big change—everything was bright—almost shocking to the eyes."

Upon arrival, the Singer family moved in with a former family friend from Łòdz. "The house was a block or two from the cliffs, and four or five houses from what I learned was Ben Gurion's house (Israel's Prime Minister). I used to ride my bike back and forth in front of the residence, trying to get a glimpse, but never saw him once. How we ended up living with these people I don't know. It was my understanding that the Israeli government had a program that obligated its citizens to take in new immigrants (for a period of time) because of the housing shortage. Israeli families housed not just Jews from Europe but people from the Arab world also."

"We lived with these people for a time, and then we moved into a place on the outskirts of Tel Aviv—or what was once the outskirts. It was a part of town that had a large Yemenite population. And that is where I went to school."

Geoffrey recalls that the area as being mostly unsettled. "There was hardly anything there but orange and lemon groves. We used to run through the groves and borrow all kinds of fruit. We were kids hanging around with other kids who had emigrated from almost every country you could imagine. We were all buddies. I would say when I look back that the whole year or so when we waited to come to America was probably the most fun I've had in my life." At eight years of age, Geoffrey entered the third grade and learned Hebrew in three months. It was the end of the school year in 1955-56, right around the time of the Suez Crisis.

Geoffrey remembers not long after his arrival it was the summertime and school closed for summer break. "We stayed up 'til all hours of the night. There was no crime and no reason to look over your shoulder. Everyone had their doors open. We would say, 'Are you decent? I am coming in.' It was a joy living this way."

Geoffrey's father, Henry, had a different experience. "While we were living in Israel, my father left for the US under some sort of visa program. He ended up living in Canada, where he had friends, and my aunt had a studio apartment available. He was doing manual work in order to send us the money in Israel. For some legal/immigration reason we had to wait nine months before we could join him."

"My father didn't work in Israel because he was unable to find a job there. It was a difficult time. There was a housing shortage. We got to Israel at the time of the Suez Crisis. Because of Eisenhower's intervention, negotiations were still underway. Israel was covered in sandbags, and food was rationed."

"Looking back, I will always be grateful for our two years in Israel. Israel was the first place I felt like I could take a deep breath. It was nothing I cognitively understood or could articulate at that time. Somehow, I understood I was in a country that was a Jewish country and that I could trust my neighbors.

"I knew I was Jewish, but I didn't understand religion. Being Jewish in Poland meant that people called me names. They laughed at me, pointing at me like I was wrong. Like there was something wrong with me." Life in Israel was a fresh breath of air for Geoffrey. He finally felt like he had a place to call home.

"After about one year living there, I dreamt of joining the Israeli special forces. I used to watch the special forces soldiers with admiration. They had no rank or insignia on their uniforms but they wore red berets. I wanted to be in the special forces so badly. I would go to the tippy top of the roof of our apartment building and stand on the edge, practicing to become a paratrooper. I looked down with half of my feet hanging over the edge and imagined what it would be like to hit the ground for the love of my country."

Despite enjoying daily life in Israel, my parents were not

religiously observant at all. About ten years before my mother died, I had a conversation with her about the Łòdz Ghetto. I asked her if she prayed to God for help from their terrible situation. My mother banged on the table with such fierce anger and said, 'We prayed, and we prayed and prayed, and nothing happened.' My father was also not observant. He used to tell us that (while living in Brooklyn) the only things that are not kosher (for the purposes of eating) are razor blades, thumb tacks, and scrap metal. When we got to the US, my parents sent me to a Yeshiva, and there I became more aware of my anxiety about being Jewish."

School in Israel was much less regimented than public school had been in Łòdz. In Łòdz there was a strict dress code: cuffs must cover the forearms; to protect the floors, house slippers were worn; children sat with hands behind their backs until the teacher arrived. In Israel, Geoffrey felt comfortable in the classroom for the first time. And he wasn't singled out.

Physical Education class was different. There, Geoffrey encountered some regimentation. "We had four or five exercises in which we had to do the same movements at the same time," Geoffrey describes. "They seemed to be training us for the military. They pounded into our brains that we must speak only Hebrew, not any other language, including Yiddish. 'Yiddish is the language of the diaspora,' they said. 'Now you have a country. Here we speak Hebrew. We have enemies all around, and our army needs to speak one language.' That was one way I realized this was my country, and that the enemy was not the Jew as it seemed to be in Poland. It was the countries that surrounded us."

"In Poland I had two bicycles—an English racer and a German dirt bike racer. My father told me to disassemble them so we could take them with us. In Israel, I put them back together with high handlebars (macho bike). Because I was curious, I rode my bike to Jaffe, in Hebrew 'Yafa.' I would ride my bike into this Arab enclave. No one really noticed me hanging around cafés (with patrons in local garb drinking Turkish coffee in little cups and smoking cigarettes). I rode my bike all over Tel Aviv.

"I didn't understand what conflict really meant. I just wanted to see what this neighborhood was like. There was no crime. We had a feeling of security. I had a tremendous feeling of freedom. We had friends who held a Passover seder with the head of the household actually lying down. It was a night to recline to celebrate freedom from slavery, like a seder should be. I did not go to synagogue. It wasn't so much Jewish as Israeli. Jewishness was the background, but we were part of a new country."

Neighborhood kids would play hide and seek until almost midnight. They played typical childhood games like marbles and soccer. Once in a while, there was a little fist fight, but unlike in Poland, these dustups had nothing to do with religion or nationality.

"At the age of ten when we left, I was so sad to leave. In my child's mind, I wouldn't get a chance to fight and possibly die for my country. And then of course there was always a female in my life. My crush in Israel was named Aviva, and she was from Yemen. She had dewy olive coloring. I can still picture her beautiful face and green eyes. On the day I was leaving Israel, all I wanted to do was kiss her goodbye. But I didn't have the courage. She was a little older than me. I was ten and she was probably twelve. She was our next-door neighbor.

"A cousin of my mother's drove us by car to Haifa, where we boarded an Italian vessel called the Paccia, an old passenger ship. We departed Haifa in the early evening hours. As I watched Haifa disappear, I knew I wouldn't be back for a very long time. Next, we would end up in Brooklyn."

Geoffrey's sister, Helen's memories of Israel were fleeting. She was too young to remember much. As she put it, "I have pieces of visions and was never quite sure if they were memories or vestiges of what my brother or mother told me that happened. In general, I remember playing and running around with other children and mostly having a good time. I vividly remember the trip on the ship from Israel to France. We were in the lower decks, and I threw up constantly—I could not tolerate the smell of Italian food that was coupled with the choppy waters."

Becoming Americans

"We came to America indigent, with all our money lost from our hard times under communist rule." My parents returned to their beginnings, working in the textile/garment business." Henry was a presser; Edith was a seamstress. "They worked on piecework. It was ¼ of a cent for this and ½ a cent for that." In the early years, the family was poor, and the neighborhood was rough. The Singers started out in Brooklyn. "It was a West Side Story in East New York, Brooklyn."

"Brooklyn in those years was a hell hole," Geoffrey's sister, Helen remembers. "We lived on the first floor of an old apartment building. Because we were above the basement and the walls had cracks, our apartment was infested with mice and roaches. We set mouse traps and if I had to go to the bathroom at night, I would take my father's shoe to kill the dozens of roaches that would scurry when I turned on the light. Crime was rampant. I can't tell you how many times I would come home from school only to find we had been burglarized. At about nine years old, I had to run away from gangs with zip guns and chains that threatened me."

"My parents worked long hours. I basically had to take care of myself and do chores around the house that would normally fall onto someone who was older. I grew up quickly."

Geoffrey said, "Helen and I went to school and rapidly became Americanized. Our finances improved, and we moved to Queens (in New York). We were introduced to Rock and Roll and teenage staples like American Bandstand. My parents loved Perry Como, Andy Williams, and Tony Bennett. We would all watch the Ed Sullivan Show. Then the unthinkable happened. Our father, Henry, was diagnosed with terminal cancer."

Geoffrey's sister, Helen, recounted, "In those days, Cancer or the big C, was a secret. We couldn't tell anyone. We didn't even tell my father that he was dying. It took him about two years to die, the last few months were the most miserable, with him suffering in pain. Hospitals did not keep terminal patients, and there was a scarcity of hospice situations. The only place was in the Bronx and run by nuns. When my father awoke in his room and saw all the images of Jesus Christ on the crucifix staring at him, he begged us to get him out. The next day we brought him home. The cancer care aide would take care of him during the day, and Geoffrey and I would take turns taking care of him at night. My mother had to sleep so she could work, as we needed the money. Henry Singer died on December 30, 1969, during my freshman year in college."

Helen continued, "A few years later, our mother moved to Toronto to be with her sister Dorka and shortly thereafter remarried. I graduated from Queens College (CUNY), remained in the New York area, and started a successful career on Wall Street in investment banking. Geoffrey moved to Los Angeles where he also enjoyed a successful career in import/export freight forwarding. We lived the American Dream—not bad for immigrant children of parents that suffered and survived through so many atrocities."

A Visit to Poland

In January of 1999, forty-nine-year-old Geoffrey made his first return trip to Poland to see the city where he was born, witness the places that had impacted his family, and find his beloved childhood nanny, Stefcia.

Additionally, Geoffrey conducted business while abroad, meeting with Polish individuals in his field. "While I was employed as an international freight forwarding executive, I considered myself more of a philosopher as I often had to untangle complicated issues. My line of business was somewhat esoteric. Early on in the cargo industry, I specialized in forwarding personal effects. I also handled logistics, sales and negotiations with airlines, steamships, railroads, and interstate trucking. I worked for five or six different companies, representing exporters and importers. I loved the business and was in it for twenty-eight years. I opened my own business in 1998, just in time for the Asian financial crisis. I had a hard time from the get-go. After my business closed, I had some time to travel.

"When I decided to go back to Poland, I began my search for our nanny, Stefcia. Stefcia pretty much raised me. She was like a second mother to me. She was very kind and a true Christian. She wore a gold crucifix necklace all the time. And she walked the walk.

"One time, the kids in the building were picking on me, and she saw it. She was crying with tears streaming from her eyes. She knocked on their parents' doors and said to them, 'Is this what you teach your children? Didn't you see what happened here during the war? How can you teach your children this?' All the time she was screaming and crying. She was with the family until we left Poland. After we left, my parents sent her money on a regular basis.

"By the time I returned, she was very old and sick, with an advanced case of diabetes. She looked much older than I expected (probably in her mid-seventies). Stefcia was extremely overweight. She couldn't move very well; it was clear she was unwell. Though she was probably somewhere around the age of my parents, she appeared much older." Geoffrey attempted to place Stefcia's age. "Let's say she was twenty years old in 1944 during the Warsaw uprising."

"I bought her some of the things she needed. I bought her an electric teapot, a microwave, a walker, and a few other things. Because I had spent that extra money (all very expensive in Poland), when I got back to LA, I only had a few dollars in my pocket. I didn't even have enough money to get a taxi home. I had to go to the ATM at the airport.

"When I began my search for Stefcia, all I had was an address, which I got from my mother. Stefcia didn't know I was coming into town." Geoffrey knocked on her door. When he first glanced at his former nanny, he found himself unable to form words as childhood memories overwhelmed him. "I was just staring at her and felt speechless. She got a little panicky. I couldn't say anything because I was completely choked up.

"She didn't recognize me. Then after one minute or so of staring at her, I realized I was making her nervous. That's when I called her by her name. I called out, 'Stefcia,' and after a moment she paused, then she recognized me. I spent three nights in her apartment. Each night we talked almost all night long. She had no family, I'm not sure why. I can tell you this: she fought in the Polish uprising in Warsaw in 1944 (the Warsaw Ghetto Uprising was led by the underground resistance). I'm not sure she was a hero, but I like to believe she was.

"How did she feel about working with a Jewish family? She was a true Christian; she didn't have a bone of hate in her body. I remember when we were leaving. She cried and cried. I remember her saying, 'My whole life will be completely different when you are gone.' We treated her very well, like one of the family. The Polish authorities wouldn't let her out. It was a communist country, but they let us out because we were Jewish and considered non-persons."

Reminiscing with Stefcia increased Geoffrey's sense of nostalgia, and he became curious about his childhood home. He dropped by the old neighborhood in Old Town, and found it was worse for wear. He hesitated briefly before knocking on the weathered front door. "I remembered just which door to knock on. And a young woman answered, holding a baby. I apologized for showing up at her door unannounced and explained my family had occupied this unit until 1956." The current tenant was captivated by Geoffrey's return from the US and invited him to come in and look around. (She shared that she had a fascination with Americans). "It was a mild January, and so I wore a light jacket with an Indiana Jones hat.

"I went into the apartment. It was completely different. They separated off extra rooms, keeping the basic structure somewhat similar, but the layout was much choppier. The windows were old. It had been elegant with high ceilings and French doors.

Most of Łòdz was built in the 1850s. It was hard to tell if it was run-down or just dreary like its surroundings.

"The young tenant's husband or boyfriend was dragging a bottle of vodka, and he could hardly stand. He was clearly inebriated and couldn't even talk. I gave her twenty US dollars, and she was so grateful. When I walked down the stairs, she ran after me, handing me a container of mace, saying, 'It's not the same as when you lived here. It's a very dangerous neighborhood at night. If you see a group of young men, cross the street.'"

"I visited both Auschwitz and Birkenau, places of my father's imprisonment. Auschwitz is the original Auschwitz, and three kilometers away (about one and a half miles) is Birkenau, which was built in 1943." Geoffrey verifies his dates with the help of Siri, discovering the death complex was built over the winter of 1941–42 and probably became active in 1943.

He comments, "It was finished near the end of '42. I was almost correct. The ghetto was emptied out from August 3 to August 28, 1944. My dad was on one of the last trains with his wife and baby. He was in Auschwitz up until mid-September.

"Auschwitz was built with as much secrecy as possible and had a fully guarded perimeter. No matter who you were, unless you had some pull somewhere, you had almost no chance of escape. I walked around there and kept on asking myself if I could have worked my way out of there. The answer was probably not. You couldn't get far as an escapee; the place was locked up. My own father was moved to Birkenau, Flossenbürg, and finally a death march, which he miraculously survived."

Geoffrey walked over to the Auschwitz train depot where the Jewish prisoners were unloaded. "The Jews were unloaded in an area covered in gravel. I know my father had to step on that gravel someplace, so I walked the entire length of gravel back and forth until I covered the entire length and width with footsteps. I told myself I don't know where, but I must have stepped somewhere where my father placed his feet."

Geoffrey purchased a book at the museum gift shop that

contained "a whole history of Auschwitz—who was in charge, how many calories were allotted to each prisoner, executions, and so on. So, when I got back to my hotel room in Krakow, I began to read, and I just went into a frenzy. Let me tell you something—it was like a frenzy I had never experienced. This cab driver took me back to the train station. He was trying to work me for extra money." Geoffrey felt so on edge after spending the day at the death camps that he fought to contain his anger, now directed toward the cab driver, who was trying to take advantage of a tourist at an unfortunate time.

Adding to his anger, Geoffrey couldn't help but notice that the driver had an ethnic German name (from his posted name plaque). "What happened in this Auschwitz area is that it was decided to make it into an exhumation camp. They ejected all the people of Polish descent from the Auschwitz complex and put in Polish ethnic Germans (the Auschwitz area has been occupied by Germans and Poles). I felt my cab driver could have been one of those or descended from someone associated with the camp." Somehow, Geoffrey was able to extract himself from his cab.

The visit to Poland had been an emotional roller coaster for Geoffrey, but the memories and feelings it stirred brought family experiences of the past to life in a new way.

Henry and Edith in NYC, 1966

Young Henry, left, circa 1936. Above, circa 1951-52

Left, Edith with Geoffrey and Helen (in stroller) on Piotrkowska St. in Lodz, Poland. Below, circa 1930, Lutz, Poland: Grandfather Pinkus Zyngier, grandmother Chaja Geclewicz and children. Henry (Henryk) is tallest, center.

Left, Helen and Geoffrey on a Baltic Sea boardwalk, circa 1955-56. Below, Henry, young Geoffrey, and Edith in the mountains of Zakopane, Poland, 1955

Below, Henry on the deck of a ship, bound to the U.S., circa 1957

Edith and Henry, above, in Lodz, Poland, circa 1946-47

Chapter Nine
Helen Singer-Katz with Son, Daniel Katz
Family Spellings: Zyngier, Zinger, Singer
A Return to Poland: Back to the Roots Trip

"My brother, Geoffrey has a better memory of our life in Poland," explains his younger sister, seventy-one-year-old Helen Singer-Katz of Northern New Jersey. "When we left Poland, I was only four years old, so I really don't have strong memories other than the ones my brother or my mother told me."

Rather than holding full-blown memories, Helen has momentary visions, instances when she can flash back to her earlier years. She believes they are a combination of early memories along with added anecdotes provided by family members.

"I'm not sure if it was Geoff or my mother who told me this story, but it goes like this: When I was still a toddler, a neighborhood kid came up to the playground and started taunting my brother. I was playing with some sort of toy in the sandbox, maybe it was a shovel. I was told that I threatened those kids and stood up for him. 'Leave him alone,' I shouted.

"In another instance of shared memory, my mother told me I would sit by the window in the apartment alongside our nanny, Stefcia, who helped take care of us. Nanny would feed me in front of the window, so I could watch everyone walk by. I was told that I made up my own names for them in Polish." Geoffrey fondly recalls his baby sister's gibberish, calling young Polish men Palepkee and young Polish women Palepczipekee.

"When I went back for a visit to Poland in 2010, nothing really jogged my memory. I had some pictures of Łòdz (of us walking in the street), of me in my carriage (perhaps in Freedom Square). I really don't have memories of Poland other than that."

Helen returned to her Polish birthplace on what she describes as a back-to-the-roots trip for her son Daniel's twenty-first birthday in 2010. One intention of her trip was genealogy tourism, a trend in which families attempt to unearth their family story by visiting places where their ancestors once lived. Helen and her husband, Michael Katz, thought Daniel had reached an appropriate age to see where his family had come from and what they had survived within recent history. "I figured he would never go to Poland or Eastern Europe on his own. (She mentions that Eastern Europe is not first on the wish list for the younger generation.) My husband's family are Holocaust survivors too, from Hungary, Czechoslovakia (now the Czech Republic), and the Ukraine area."

While Daniel (Dan) agrees he may not have ventured to Poland on his own, the young journalist, currently serving as Vice President of News for Texas Public Radio was eager to make connections with his late grandparents. "The trip did help me connect a little bit more. "There's a difference between learning about something in a history book versus actually experiencing it. "You look at those pictures in books and watch movies like Schindler's List that are so powerful (and other notable films like The Pianist), and you feel an emotional tug. But physically, being in those places is an experience on a whole other level. There's a difference between hearing about the tracks that go in and out of Auschwitz or looking at them in a textbook in school and seeing the tracks that your grandparents trekked upon. Learning about the Holocaust intellectually is very hard to do when all four of your grandparents are survivors…"

Dan said, "All of my family members being so closely tied to the Holocaust, it wasn't something I really liked to hear and talk about, but once you see it, it changes everything for you." Dan shares that as an adolescent he was more interested in emulating sports heroes like Derek Jeter or Dan Marino than the Baal Shem Tov (an important historical Jewish figure and founder of Hasidic Judaism). He notes that the Holocaust and suffering are hard to comprehend when you grow up with a comfortable American lifestyle.

"I just wanted to mask the feelings of being a third-generation survivor, as well as being a first-generation American. I wanted to be thought of as just an American. I wanted to play sports and do my thing, hang out with friends. This connection wasn't something I was necessarily seeking." Having a Jewish education and attending a K-8 Jewish day school helped form Dan's Jewish identity. He feels that his trip to Eastern Europe gave his Judaism a sense of history and meaning.

Through family lore, Dan had learned that he shared many qualities with his maternal grandfather, Henry Singer. Dan was eager to feel Henry's presence as he toured Poland. He comments, "My grandfather and I never met. He died of lung cancer before I was born." While visiting Łòdz, Dan was treated to snippets of memory from his mother. When the family walked past the Hotel Grand, an elegant hotel built in 1888 (not as elegant at the time of their visit but is currently well-reviewed), Helen recalled that this was where her father had played cards with his buddies. "I felt a little connection at that moment. People tell me I'm like him in some ways. He was a runner in the Polish army. I did cross country running in high school. I'm pretty tall and don't have a natural runner's body. But when I was going on these multiple mile runs, I felt I was connecting with him."

"My grandfather was kind of a natural leader from what I gathered. Everyone liked him. I think it's one of the reasons he was given a position of authority in the ghetto, and did well in the military and in business, too. Like him, I try to live with empathy and curiosity, while learning my way around an organization. I'm an incredibly hard worker (like all my grandparents). I like to think that I'm making my grandfather proud."

"Even though I look very American and feel very American, I am the first generation in my family to be born here.

The Katz family met up in Warsaw with Michael's cousins, Shlomo and Ronit, who are Israelis with family from the Ukraine.

The group drove through various parts of Poland, Slovakia, Hungary, as well as the western part of Ukraine. "My son was attending a course in Paris on producing documentaries. We flew to Paris, picked him up, then headed to Warsaw."

Helen comments that the western part of Ukraine they visited close to the Romanian/Moldovan border has not been invaded by the war thus far (as of September 2022). Dan adds from a journalist's perspective, "Whether or not an area has been invaded, everyone in Ukraine has been touched by the war. Are there buildings on fire? Maybe not. But are refugees coming through? Is everything really expensive? Is it hard for them to live right now? Yes. Everyone there is touched by it."

"We went as far as a city called Chernivtsi (There are many spellings for this formerly Jewish area), known as one of Western Ukraine's main cultural centers," notes Helen. Shlomo's family was from there. Michael's family was from Mukachevo (Mukacheve since 2017), Ukraine, 30 kilometers from the Hungarian border. Jews called it Munkatsh (Yiddish name), but it went by many different names and spellings; it has been part of Hungary and Russia at different times.

"The visit to Ukraine was one of the best parts of our trip, Helen continued. The areas the family visited were mostly rural and surprisingly undeveloped. "We went from small town to small town, noting the old women in their babushkas sitting by the roadside selling an apple or a potato." The picturesque scene was complete with ancient wagons and barrels full of hay. Helen notes that they did not visit the big cities like Kyiv. Instead, they were looking for places with (Shlomo's) familial connections.

An important part of this back-to-the-roots trip was to spend time in Poland, especially Auschwitz, to gain first-hand knowledge of what had happened in those places. "Both my father and my husband's mother, Vera Katz, survived Auschwitz. We believed our son needed to connect to that experience."

Helen was surprised by Poland's appearance, as well as how it felt to be there. In her mind, the country appeared gray, dingy, and old like her mother had described it. "However, visually, Warsaw was all built up and looked like any thriving city. Lòdz, where I was born, was more run-down, especially the neighborhood where we had lived. The architecture had been stunning, like the 5th Avenue of its day before the war. But when we arrived, half the buildings were still burnt out. Windows were boarded up and there were graffiti with swastikas all over the place." The other side of town was redeveloped with a square and a modern city center. The older section where they had lived was more of a slum.

Dan comments, "My family lived right off the main street, Piotrkowska Street, which went through the center of Lòdz. There were still some buildings that looked right out of World War II, but there was also new development. We saw a former factory that had become a mixed-use development. I don't think Lòdz was ever known as a super elegant place. It was a manufacturing city. It reminded me of the rougher outskirts of New York or New Jersey."

In Lòdz, the Katz family tried to find evidence of the former ghetto but were only able to find a dilapidated cemetery (which most likely had been the cemetery for the ghetto residents). Helen had been hoping to locate the graves of her grandparents, but the cemetery office was closed, and she did not know the location of their graves. "It was so overgrown that only a few graves were visible. Even if I had the location of their grave sites, I would not have been able to find them because it was such a large cemetery and so unkempt with overgrown grass and weeds."

Dan commented, "We weren't really able to find many relics of the former ghetto. Everywhere we had visited—Prague, Budapest, Warsaw—there were statues and pieces of living history. Not so much in Lòdz." Dan acknowledges the other cities they visited were larger and appeared to have a greater recovery than Lòdz. "Communism wasn't very kind to Lòdz."

A Land of Contradictions

Helen describes Poland as "a land of contradictions," explaining, "I speak Polish poorly, but I understand the language pretty well. Polish is an interesting language—very proper and polite. I find the nature of the language to be contradictory, though I am not sure if that is the right word." To Helen, the propriety of the language belied the brutality and racism against the Jewish people during the war.

She comments, "I never liked the Polish people. My mother used to say she would never go back. I had a deep hatred for what happened there and for the complicity in what happened to my family. For the most part, my entire family was wiped out—if not in the Łòdz Ghetto, then in Auschwitz."

During their visit, Helen felt that she was treated fine. "We were Americans, and they wanted our money." I was very careful and spent as little money as possible. I wasn't going to give them anything other than what was necessary for lodging and food. That was my resentment for my own loss and the loss of so many others. Along with members of my family, they lost a lot of brain power and accomplished people."

They visited Jewish cemeteries (like the one in Łòdz) throughout Eastern Europe to honor those who were lost. "We visited Jewish cemeteries everywhere. We visited ones in Prague, Warsaw, and Munkatsh." In Warsaw, they found the monument marking the location of the Warsaw Ghetto. With the help of a guide, they saw a remaining ten-foot wall. They also lit a candle on behalf of the six million lost. After visiting the renowned factory in Krakow owned by Oskar Schindler, it seemed like everywhere the family went was associated with death.

The visit to Auschwitz brought up complex emotions for the family. By the time she arrived in Auschwitz, Helen was overcome with all the loss that surrounded the Jewish people as well as the personal losses suffered by her own family. There, she felt a deep connection to her late father, who had survived the camp but lost his wife and baby daughter. "We also went to Birkenau from there. It was heart-wrenching. I don't know how anyone can come out of those places unchanged or unbroken. (That's how I sensed the way my parents felt. I thought they felt broken.)"

While visiting a barrack in Auschwitz, Helen experienced a moment of panic and questioned how anyone was able to survive imprisonment. "One of the barracks where prisoners had lived had been converted into an exhibit, kind of a mini museum. All the rest of our group had wandered off, and it was only me and Daniel left in this small, dark bunker. "I just freaked out. I felt like they were going to lock the door and leave us there. I grabbed Daniel and just ran out. That's how paranoid I was in that place."

Dan remembers that shared moment with his mother. "I recall how dark it was in that bunker. It was incredibly scary. Having been to Auschwitz and then Birkenau, it gets worse and worse as you get deeper into the camps. When you come through the gates of Auschwitz you see the infamous sign 'Work Makes You Free.' The original Auschwitz was set up as a military camp. As you go deeper in, you are exposed to darker things, like the exhibit of shoes belonging to the murdered souls." Dan mentioned reading powerful and heartbreaking signage and literature that accompanied the exhibits. "As you walk farther into the complex—to Birkenau—you see things (like scarred wooden barracks meant for sleeping, basically wooden shelves, a crematorium) that stripped humanity from the prisoners. The more we saw, the darker it was."

Dan explains that his emotions came out later that night. "Our trip took place when smart phones had just become popular. I had my Blackberry at the time. I remember reading an article on my phone about the latest flare up against the Israeli people. (An international leader had decried that Israelis were the children of Hitler.) For a politician to make a comment like that in the year 2010, this showed how little progress had been made regarding worldwide antisemitism. It hit me very hard while staying in Krakow and spending the day in Auschwitz. It made me incredibly angry. I am trained as a journalist to keep a steady presence and not let my opinion influence anything. It made me feel that at this moment I was living, my family's place in history was in danger of being repeated. It's still going on today."

Family Reunions

Reuniting with family brought some lighter moments to the Katz's family travels. On a happier occasion, the family met up with Michael's cousin who lives in Ukraine. His daughter, Svetlana, took them deeper into Ukraine. Helen notes that it was helpful that Svetlana spoke the language, though Helen was able to pick up some conversation because of her Polish background. "We celebrated both Daniel's and Svetlana's birthdays during the trip. It was a wonderful trip in that regard, getting to know our family, but I don't think I would ever want to go back. I just needed to see it. Geoff had been back a couple of times, I think. It was important for my son to see these places and to experience his family's history from my side and from my husband's side. My father died when I was eighteen, so Daniel never had a chance to know him. He knew my mother. She was already older. And he grew up with Michael's parents."

"We took Dan on regular visits to see my mom, who lived in Toronto, and to see Michael's parents, who lived in South Florida. Michael's parents were more youthful and more involved. They were able to travel and visit us as well."

Remembering Edith (Edzia)

"I called my maternal grandmother Bubbie." Dan remembers her as a "classy lady, always very well dressed, stylish even." He recalls that fashion was important to her, and that she had made hats for a living after the war.

"Bubbie was very cultured. We didn't come from amazing

wealth, but she understood the finer things and life and wanted to expose her family to those things. She was very loving. While I always felt her love for me, she did not necessarily know how to relate to me as a kid growing up in the '90s. Though she was quiet and reserved, Daniel enjoyed the times when she put down her guard. "You would be surprised to know that she was a Three Stooges fan. She would just crack up, watching it on TV."

"There was a feeling when she was around me of a grandmother being around her only grandson." Dan explains that while sometimes she lacked the words to express herself (and physically she was limited by her age and her health), he felt her unconditional love. "She passed away in 2002. My mom tells me she willed herself to live until my bar mitzvah and died soon after."

New Perspectives on Family

Helen explains the evolution of the family surname, which was Zyngier (also listed as Zinger on some prewar and wartime documents). "After we became naturalized, we became known as Singer. Then, when I married, I hyphenated it to Singer-Katz. My parents changed our spelling because they wanted it to sound more American. They changed my first name, which was Halina. I wish they would have kept it. Halina was a beautiful name. Helen is just ordinary.

"I had no idea I had a great uncle [Sandi Solomon's grandfather, Meyer Singer] who came to the states in the early 1920s. I was kind of in shock after receiving an email from Sharon Fleitman. Geoff and I had different reactions to her outreach. He was angry at my parents for not telling us we had more cousins/family. I thought to myself, Why wouldn't they tell us?

"Then, I started talking to other people with similar experiences. I surmised that a newly arrived family of greenhorns (like mine) may have seemed burdensome to their Americanized relatives.

"Everyone has a different immigration story. I am amazed

how individual our stories are, while at the same time sharing many commonalities, like the feeling of isolation. I started understanding that my parents must have felt very isolated. I felt I understood them a little better and even felt sorry for them. I think I talked Geoff down a little bit, and he let his anger go.

"We were in shock but also extremely happy. I always wanted more family. We don't have a lot of family. Since we first made contact with Sharon and her husband, Eric, we have taken a trip to Atlanta to meet them. We have also spent time together on Zoom and Facetime. We keep up with Eric's mother, Sandi, who is my second cousin. I feel close to her even though we are years apart. I am directly on the genealogy line with Sandi. Our grandparents were siblings (Sandi's grandfather and my grandfather). But I am closer to Eric Solomon's age."

Helen's son, Dan concurs that connecting with the new cousins has brought happiness to the family. "We met up with Eric and Sharon at their son's wedding, where we also met Sandi. It was the middle of the pandemic, and I hadn't seen my parents or my Uncle Geoff in a while, almost a year at that point. My parents had been doing a lot of Zoom meetings with the cousins, but I was so busy with work, I hadn't gotten a chance to really know them."

Dan continued, "We have a very small family—especially for my mom and uncle. They were mostly shocked because it was not what they had been told or understood. To me, it was very cool because they were warm people, very interested. Second cousins may not be meaningful for many people, but our family was so small that it makes a big difference.

"It didn't feel like I was meeting people for the first time. There was an unexpected closeness. "We had just met, and Sandi was already texting me Happy birthday, Chag Sameach (a wish for a joyous celebration in Hebrew) when there's a holiday. I am not always great about getting back to her, but she never takes it personally. She is a very positive person, a trait in common with the rest of our family."

Viewing Henryk Ross Exhibit Brings Up Old Memories

In 2017, Helen accompanied her cousin Mirla Geclewicz (also related from Helen's father's side, but from the grandmother not the grandfather), to Boston to view an exhibit featuring the well-known Łòdz photographer Henryk Ross. Ross had been a Łòdz Ghetto resident with the assigned job (as a prisoner/slave laborer) of taking propagandist photos within the ghetto. While Ross took many propagandist photos of Ghetto prisoners, he also took thousands of illegal pictures showing poverty and suffering within the ghetto walls, with the hope he would have the opportunity to share them with the world. When Ross was sent to Auschwitz during the ghetto liquidation process, he buried thousands of photo negatives for safekeeping.

Helen said, "We took a train together to Boston. The presenters projected around two thousand photos on a screen. My cousin searched for a photo of her father while he was a ghetto resident and believes she found one. She sent that picture along with later photos of her father to forensic specialists to confirm his identity and received a report of a 95 percent probability that it was him. She later published a memoir of her parents' survival and postwar experiences titled The Birds Sang Eulogies with this picture of her father on the cover. I was looking for my mother's picture. I identified a few photos that looked like her, but I was never sure. The pictures were small and grainy."

Geoffrey also voices appreciation for the photography of Henryk Ross: "There are books that have collections of his pictures, and I have those books. His images give an idea of what it was like to be in the ghetto. I was surprised he wasn't caught, given the tremendous risks he took. The most interesting photo that I recall is one of Rumkowski in conversation with Hitler. That was the real thing. It was a combination of what I was reading and the pictures that he took. Made a full picture. Made it all jibe."

In reflecting about her mother, Helen remarks, "My mother

had few stories to share about the ghetto. I do recall her sharing this anecdote about her sister, with whom she survived life in the ghetto. My mother [Helen called her "Mommy" after moving to the US at the age of six] told me that food was so scarce that Dorka would smuggle carrots into their living quarters in her underwear. That made a pretty unforgettable image. However, Geoffrey is not familiar with that story, speculating, 'I would say it could have happened once or maybe two times in the beginning. The ghetto was closed off completely by May Day. No sewer system, which made smuggling very difficult (not to mention all the sentry posts).'

"Geoff would remember better, but I think Dorka had typhus, and my mom refused to send her to the hospital. She knew if her sister was sent to the hospital, she would be dead. Somehow, my mother kept her alive at great risk, without catching it herself.

"Growing up as a second-generation survivor—and I think Geoff and a lot of other second-generation survivors felt the same way—I did not want to hear what happened because it was so sad, and so personal. I wanted to be in denial. I was in denial. I wanted to be a kid. I wanted to be an American and live my life.

"Also, my parents tried not to talk about their lives during the war. They talked about it between themselves and with friends. I overheard some things. Generally speaking, I did not want to know. And I didn't want to know because of the whole denial process. I knew the horrible impact it had on our lives. That I knew. Here I am a kid in a new country trying to fit in, and I didn't want to hear about the trauma my parents had experienced. They never told us a lot of the details.

"It wasn't until I was in my twenties that I started facing up to who I was and what my background was. And then I got Geoff involved when I went to a Second-Generation Conference at UCLA in December 1987. (Today Second-Generation Conferences are mostly online, and Helen keeps connected through Facebook chats.) I made him come and experience it with me. "After attending that conference, Helen became more at peace with her background and her parents' tragic early life. "I felt more at home with who I was and where my parents came from. I began to accept that their dysfunctionality as people stemmed from the experiences they went through.

"When we attended the conference in California, the movement to bring descendants of Holocaust survivors together was in its early stages. People our age were just starting to come to grips with how their parents' traumatic experiences affected their own lives." These gatherings continue to proliferate under various names and are sponsored by different umbrella organizations. There Helen learned she had much in common with other children of survivors (so much in common that she met her husband Michael at the conference). Like Helen, they felt like they carried a heavy burden on behalf of their parents. "I felt like I was taking care of my parents and found myself in the caretaking role. When they first came here, they were working such long hours and didn't know the language well. I felt a responsibility for doing more things for them. I filled out applications for them and took on adult responsibilities, even as a child as I had better facility with English." It was a relief when other conference members said they felt similarly."

She explains further, "A lot of these people (survivors) who went through their formative years in ghettos and camps, who lost their parents early, didn't have the guidance growing up they may have wanted and needed. Some people came out from the darkness stronger, like the well-known author and survivor Elie Wiesel. Some people were just impacted emotionally in ways that were very detrimental to their lives. I think my parents were among those people. Everybody has some kind of problem. But when you suffer from trauma for so long, it exacerbates whatever else is going on in your life. The fact that my parents persevered after what they experienced inspires me. They were able to have a family (for my father, a second family after horrifically losing his first) and own and conduct business. They bravely moved around the world—to countries where they didn't speak the languages—to better the lives of their children. That took a lot of courage.

"Over the last twenty years, I have begun to see how much courage that took despite their personal issues."

"My mother was a businesswoman when my parents met at her millinery business. My father went to work for her and her sister, Dorka. He fell in love with my mother, and they got married. My father had a previous family that perished. I never knew his first wife's name until now—thank you Sharon! He never spoke about it. The only thing I knew about his first family is that he had a daughter named Chaya or Chana (Chaja on the Auschwitz registry). She was named after my grandmother (Henry Singer's mother, also Chaja). This is what my father told us: she was killed in Auschwitz when she was two, although Sharon found data entries showing that she was only six or eight months old. We have different information, and I can't prove it one way or another. I would go with Sharon's documentation.

"We would have discussions here and there. Our talks were so sad and difficult. That is exactly what my father would say, 'My life is sad and difficult.' I remember my father told me that he wanted to have a little girl. Geoffrey was born first. My mother always told me she didn't want another kid because Geoffrey was so sickly when he was a baby. There was a time when I felt that I might have been a replacement for my father's first daughter (we were both named after his mother). And I can see why he may have felt that way." She comments that she does not feel like that today.

Helen's mother was "not very communicative," she says, though certainly not antisocial. Helen attributes her mother's lack of openness to her tragic young adult years when she was imprisoned in the ghetto. "My mother was highly educated. My father was not. In that regard they were a mismatch. My mom took me to plays. She was a clothes horse, dressed meticulously, always in the height of fashion—ahead of the crowd. When miniskirts came into style, she force me to wear them even though I didn't want to! She would buy me beautiful clothes, and we would go to the best shoe stores. My mother would take me to a store in New York called the 34th Street Bootery. That was the place to go shopping for shoes.

"I always had the best in terms of how I looked because that's what my mother valued. For my father, it was being fed. He was the cook of the family. His father was a baker, and so he loved to cook. We always had the best cuts of meat and chicken. We were always well-fed and well-dressed."

Helen wonders if her mother's interest in fashion stemmed from her forced labor as a seamstress while living in the ghetto, where she made hats. Perhaps her training there led her to become a milliner after the war. "I have many unanswered questions because many survivors (like my mother) were disinclined to share; there are a lot of missing pieces.

"I vacillate back and forth, saying to myself, I've got to get more into this and to do more research like Sharon did. I really admire what she's done."

Jewish Identity

"I remember snippets of being in Israel but very little. I can recall images of traveling to the US and Canada—images that just pop in. I may remember some things because my brother told me about them.

"I remember that Israel was great for us kids. We were always in the streets playing and doing. It was fun. Geoff loved Israel, and he was very unhappy to leave. Israel was a stopping point to the US for my parents. They never intended to stay there and actually did not like it. My mother was unhappy there. She said, 'Everybody knew everyone else's business.' She was a private person. I didn't realize how much Geoffrey hated coming here. We didn't really talk about this stuff when we were younger. Only as we've gotten older have a lot of these things come out. We didn't have a choice. We were little children and went where our parents took us. I don't remember the hardships, and there were hardships. I just remember playing with kids. Then, when I was about six years old, we left Israel.

"I knew I was Jewish. When I came to the US, for the longest time I didn't feel like an American or very assimilated, even though I spoke English fluently. I felt American, but at the same time I didn't. There was a duality of acceptance and nonacceptance. I think many Jewish people felt this way. There was an inside and an outside.

"A lot of people feel that dichotomy. As a child of Holocaust survivors, I was sensitive to any kind of discrimination or division. That feeling faded once we moved to Queens. We settled in Brooklyn first and then moved to Queens. Our neighborhood in Queens was pretty Jewish, and I felt acclimated.

"Though I didn't experience a lot of persecution, I always carried this thought in the back of my mind, I have to be ready to flee. I have always felt that way. More so today with what's going on in the world and in this country. For a long time, Helen struggled with placing funds in investment accounts because the money was not immediately available. "You can't take your money out on demand. That's why many Jews in unstable countries hold onto diamonds and jewelry. You can just take them. My inner voice has always said, Be ready to run and to take your assets with you.

"I have always felt I was Jewish. Mainly because we were children of Holocaust survivors or were persecuted ourselves. Geoff has pointed out that perhaps discrimination has made me feel more Jewish. However, we were never highly observant. My husband Michael's parents became more observant, or felt closer to God, following their family devastation during the Holocaust, whereas my parents were just the opposite. The only thing I did observe was going to say Yizkor for my grandparents during the High Holidays. When I was a child, I remember the enjoyment of showcasing my new dress at holiday services. That was the extent of my Jewishness.

"It wasn't until my mid-twenties that I started thinking more about my Jewish identity. Not necessarily my belief in God, because I go back and forth with that, but more like a cultural, ethical, community-oriented kind of a thing. A sense of belonging. And that I wouldn't want to be anything else."

When it came time to pass on a Jewish identity to her son, Daniel, Helen raised her son as the legacy of Holocaust survivors (on both sides). "I think he was very aware of that when we took him to Auschwitz. I don't know if that was wrong of me. There is a psychiatrist who specializes in trauma in relation to survivors. She says trauma is transmitted through the generations. Maybe I passed on too much trauma. On the other hand, I believe growing up with that knowledge has made him a better person. We all have to understand where we are from. I think he knows, and he's very sensitive to that. He went to Jewish Day School. I can't transmit Jewishly to him because I didn't know it.

Dan concurs that having a Jewish education, attending a K-8 Jewish day school, helped form his Jewish identity. Additionally, he feels that his trip to Eastern Europe gave his Judaism a sense of history and meaning.

"I sent him to Jewish school so he could have the knowledge to make his own decisions regarding religion. He's like us. We don't really observe Shabbat, but he knows who he is and where he is from." Helen notes that during Daniel's bar-mitzvah year they attended Shabbat services for an entire school year. "I have learned a lot since then. I was actually very grateful for that.

"When our mother passed away, I said kaddish—the mourner's prayer— for almost a year. I found it to be very good for my soul. I learned a lot about Judaism in the process. It is a rich, beautiful religion, but to me it is more a sense of community, ethics, and identity. Belief in God, I still don't know. I believe there is something out there. Growing up in the 1960s, we believed that God was in everyone. I try to live my life in a moral and ethical way."

Helen never asked her parents whether they prayed during

their time in the ghetto. "That's why a lot of people lost their faith. It's very strange. Some survivors gained more faith; others lost theirs. Everyone's experience is quite different."

Helen celebrates all the major holidays. "For Rosh Hashanah and Yom Kippur, I go to synagogue. For the other holidays, sometimes I do, sometimes I don't. She also has devoted time giving back to her local Jewish community. "I also became active in the Jewish community charities. I like to make things better for people, for the Jewish community, for people who are at risk or who have nothing. I was able to participate in several missions to Israel, which gave me a love for that country that I never had before."

"Geoffrey and I want to thank Sharon for her superb detective work and for finding us. We are also grateful to Sandi for supporting this project and bringing our stories to life. Most of all, we are happy to have found our warm and welcoming family."

Left, Monica in her later teens. Below, right, Monica in the yard as a baby.

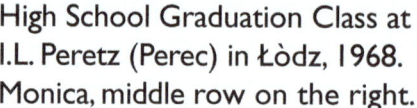

High School Graduation Class at I.L. Peretz (Perec) in Łòdz, 1968. Monica, middle row on the right.

Above, Monica (right) with father, brother Ignac, and mother. Right, parents Fajgla and Uszer Bialostocki. Below, Monica on motorcycle, age four, with parents. Below right, Monica with brother Ignac and their mother.

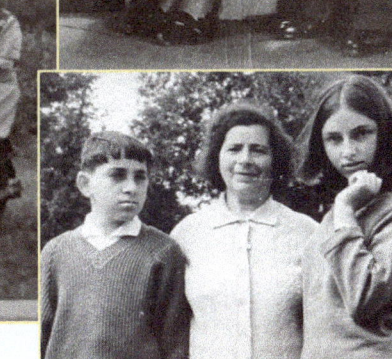

Chapter Ten
Monica Bialostocki Gutman
Family Surnames and Spellings: Wites, Perelstein

"**I was born Golda Bialostocki** in Lòdz in December 1950. Somewhere along the way, I became Monica Gutman. Post-war Poland was a place of relative peace and prosperity but many of us Jews had reasons to believe that Poles "drink antisemitism with their mother's milk." Of course many do—but not all—and I experienced both sides of this spectrum. As a young child, I sometimes heard from playmates that I can't play with them because Jews killed Jesus. When I got older and went to college, I had many friends, and my Jewishness was never an issue. But before I entered college, I spent eleven years between ages seven to eighteen, in a school named after a Jewish writer I. L. Peretz, a second home to mostly Jewish children. This school was a microcosm that shaped me and gave me a realistic introduction to the real world. There I witnessed and understood that kids with distinguishable qualities such as good looks or talents were prized—rewarded—and recipients of extra attention from adults.

"The school was a three-story building situated at an intersection of two bustling streets. This meant that even though it was a school, no provisions were made for a playground. Recesses were spent in hallways or in classrooms where we hastily and frantically caught up on homework, finished writing an essay, or read a paragraph in a history book. We didn't see trees or flowers on a regular basis unless we visited one of a handful of parks.

"Some of my classmates knew Russian as their first language and Polish as second. This was so because their parents waited out the war in Soviet Russia, then repatriated bringing with them their young families. They treated Poland as a steppingstone before moving on to Israel, USA, and Canada. This meant that my class size shrank from fifty students at its peak to ten before (at) graduation in 1968. With class size shrinking, so were opportunities to find and forge friendships. In the ever-dwindling pool of girls to hang out with, I found my best friend. She joined our school in eighth grade when her family relocated from Legnica to Łòdz. Years later, she shared with me how hard it was for her to be the outsider, the new kid, lonely and insecure. But her loneliness was the perfect match for my own sense of loneliness, and thus a lifelong friendship was born.

"Our teachers were a mix of older Jewish and younger Polish educators. Needless to say, the younger ones free from war scars were more fun and emotionally accessible. We were not taught time management, financial literacy, or healthy habits such as swimming. We didn't have counselors or psychologists to help us sort things out. There was little to no intervention in behavioral or academic deficiencies. Still, it was home, and together with the TSKZ Club, it was a place to hone social skills, engage in extracurricular activities, and sometimes—maybe—find your first love."

Monica Bialostocki Gutman bears an uncanny physical resemblance to her long-lost cousin, Sandi Solomon. Although they are about ten years apart, with Sandi being the elder, their blue eyes, fair coloring, and strawberry blond hair with similar cuts (above-the-shoulder bobs) scream family resemblance. While the two have yet to meet in person, Monica said, "When I saw Sandi, not in person but through pictures on Facebook, my first impression was that she looks like my mom."

Monica comments that her blonde hair and blue eyes contrasted with her family members' dark hair and dark eyes. She expressed her enthusiasm over her shared traits with her newfound cousin. "It was always thought that I looked like my dad; and my brother, Ignacy, looked more like my mom with a big head of black hair and long eyelashes. He was always getting compliments, and I was jealous!"

(Not surprisingly) Monica Gutman is related to American-born cousin Sandi Solomon through her mother (on Sandi's paternal side). Monica's mother, Fajgla Wites, stayed side-by-side with her sister during the war, much like the mother and aunt of Geoffrey Bar-Lev, cousins from Sandi Solomon's maternal side. Monica shares that her mother and her sister were like twins. "They stood by each other during the war when life was hell. And after, as well."

Monica's parents, both Holocaust survivors were open about their Jewish faith. "I remember my mom's diligence about Passover, always removing the chametz (breadcrumbs, products of wheat, barley, oats, and the like are forbidden during Passover) and having only matzah in the house. Chanukah was a happy celebration with small gifts from Israel like candies and apples. My mother was very religious about Yom Kippur." But as residents of a communist country, their religious practice had to remain private. Public display could be risky.

Monica and her family were surrounded by non-Jews. She comments, "Our neighbors were mostly not Jewish. Not everybody was very friendly. However, we did not feel at risk for violence. Sometimes you could feel derision, especially for the religious Jews who wore their Jewishness on the outside (like the curls or pais worn by the ultra-orthodox). The official stance of the government was 'There was no religion, whether it was Christian or Jewish.'"

Monica's parents did not meet until after the war. Her father, Uszer Bialostocki, grew up in a little town near Warsaw called Naciaz. Her mother, Fajgla/Fela Wites had lived in Stopnica, a town in southern Poland with a large Jewish population. According to Wikipedia, Stopnica was completely destroyed in World War II, "with not a single house standing."

Monica learned from her cousin Sandi about "a society from Stopnica, known as the Stopnitzer Society," which is like a club in which people stay in touch and keep memories alive. To this day, Sandi Solomon is a member of the Stopnica Young Men's

Benevolent Society. Its original mission was to help immigrants to the US from Stopnica, Poland. Today it maintains and provides Jewish burial plots and offers aid to select Jewish charities. Sandi believes her grandfather, Isaac Torgovnick, was an original member and officer of the Stopnitzer Society and a past president. Her father, Nathan, was also an active member and his bio can be found on the organization's website. At this time, Monica has not been in touch with the Stopnitzer Society, which has a presence on Facebook and (has at least in the past) had a physical presence in New York and Florida. Monica would like to touch base but feels "internet connections are not the same."

Monica recalls conversations about daily life in Stopnica between her mother and her sister, Aunt Jadzia. "I really don't have exact details, but I understood that they lived in a Jewish bubble. There wasn't much mixing with the Polish population. Growing up, she kept the traditions, and this is how I know them. When there was Passover, the cleaning was thorough, as it was in my childhood.

Monica mentions that brother, Ignacy, married a Polish woman and travels to Poland often. On a recent trip, he visited Stopnica, which has been rebuilt since the war, only this time without Jews. "Ignacy introduced himself to an official at city hall, explaining he wanted to trace his mother's history. A friendly lady told him some not so friendly news: "I'm sorry to tell you but there is nothing left." (Of the records or the original town.)

When the Germans were in Stopnica in September of 1939, they burned everything; all the buildings were wooden, so all were destroyed. Unfortunately, there is nothing to see in Stopnica that sheds light on my family's history. An article I read says that there is not even one little plaque acknowledging all the Jews who were killed there. Stopnica was about fifty per cent Jewish before the war. Why is there nothing acknowledging the pain that so many people went through? I can remember through my mother that this little town was like a Jewish haven, somewhat like a ghetto, but in a positive way. Because my mom spoke Yiddish almost to the exclusion of Polish, she read papers in Yiddish, talked to neighbors in Yiddish, and was allowed to live Jewishly in a land where Jews were pariahs.

Monica Bialostocki Gutman was born in Łòdz in 1950. "I was my parents' first child; my brother, Ignacy, came along almost five years later." The young family first lived in a "tiny, tiny" apartment. Postwar times were hard, and the Bialostockis shared their small dwelling with another family. "That family also had a child, so there were six people in two rooms divided by a little hallway with a kitchen. It was very cramped. It was not very long after the war, so the situation was still dire. The buildings were neglected. I remember there were a lot of Jewish families around me. It was like a ghetto (unofficially) without the negative connotation. "It seemed to me in the years after the war, we didn't have (as much) antisemitism because of the new system. Families stuck together. They lived on the same streets often within a mile or half a mile. We lived in what you would call downtown. In Europe it is called Centrum. My family lived almost smack in the heart of the city near the main drag called Piotrowska. Freedom Square is the heart of the city, and most Jews lived nearby. Then we had an epicenter, with a school."

Following the liberation of Łòdz in January 1945, Jewish survivors had begun to return from labor and death camps. Some hid in the forests; some drifted to areas that had been liberated already. Other survivors returned to Łòdz temporarily, hoping to find missing relatives and possibly to recover their homes and other properties. The war left many homeless, alone in the world, and penniless. After the war, many Jews settled around Łòdz rather than return to their small towns or shtetls. With postwar Warsaw nearly destroyed, Łòdz became a temporary Jewish center. While some Jews pursued hopes of going to Israel or the United States, others, like the Bialostockis stayed in Łòdz. They expected that the new socialist order would deliver at least some of the equity it promised. A Jewish Committee was founded to create organizations, jobs, schools, and housing openings.

Monica describes some of the community structures instituted in postwar. "There was a Jewish school and a Jewish club where Jewish families went to socialize, and some even found employment. I believe it was subsidized by American money. This club was government sanctioned and separate from our religious activities at our small synagogue. The club, known as the TSKZ was a place for community activities and celebrations. I remember celebrating the anniversary of the First Russian Revolution of 1905 [an uprising followed by reforms that nevertheless foreshadowed the 1917 Russian Revolution]. We would dress up in our school uniforms, and we were all given parts to recite. It was total propaganda, but at the time, it was what we knew, and (as young children) we loved the celebrations.

"The TSKZ was an organization with a mission to promote Jewishness—Jewish culture, education, and the Yiddish language. Quite a few Jewish families made a living out of this, too. They employed many people. The focus was on the younger generation. There were artistic venues, and they taught trades. The fact that this was sanctioned was a bit ironic because these same people had erased most of the Jews from the population. Still, we were triumphing. We were still there. There were houses of worship—not many but a couple.

"The I. L. Peretz School and the Jewish Club were a home to many. As you can imagine, the remaining Jewish families felt alienated postwar. My parents, for example, didn't speak the Polish language very well. They mostly spoke Yiddish and grew up enmeshed in the Jewish culture. Our parents tried to make their own Jewish bubble. As children we didn't know anything else."

The I. L. Peretz school provided Monica a place of security and solace. "The teachers at the school were very loving. Many had no children or had lost their children in the camps and were eager to share their love and affection. The school was established in the late 1940s. It was basically run by Jewish teachers, Holocaust survivors. Some of them were from Russia and became indoctrinated with communist ideals. Despite some of the teachers' personal beliefs, the school had local autonomy from the communist party, and we were not indoctrinated with communist ideology."

Jewish Theater

"Jewish theater was a big part of our cultural life," Monica says. "Even though the theater was based in Warsaw, the troupe frequently traveled. Łòdz was a big city and not very far, so they would have touring performances regularly. Ida Kaminska was a world-famous actress and a legend. When she came for a performance, it electrified the Jewish community. And my mom was a big fan." Ida Kaminska, who started her acting career in Russia, moved to Warsaw where she established Jewish theaters, first with her husband and later, on her own. After the war she returned to Warsaw.

Monica relates memories around going to the theater with her mother when she was a child and teenager. "My mom was not a glamorous person; she was not interested in elegance. She was really a hard worker. As a child, she had grown up on a farm and came from hardy peasant stock. She was very physical as a young person, trimming the trees in the orchard and fishing from a nearby pond. Because she grew up on the land, she was very down to earth. I always saw my mom very busy and stressed." Self-care was nonexistent for a postwar working mother. "But when the theater came to town, she never missed a show, and I always accompanied her. I loved taking in those rare moments when I saw my mother relaxed and beautiful."

Typically, Monica's mother carried an everyday tote that was large and disorganized, but she brought out a special purse for nights at the theater. "When she went to the theater, my mother carried a lovely little purse that I can practically feel even today; the leather—kid leather—was soft like silk to the touch. It had a beautiful closure that I have never seen replicated. This memory is so strong in my mind. I wish I could find a purse like that one on eBay or Amazon. As a child, when I opened this small purse, the fragrance of perfume wafted from inside, reminding me of our theater nights. The purse held her dressy lipstick. When she wore that, she radiated. I loved going to the theater. Not only because of the show but because of the chocolate mints my mother would buy (and other little special treats). Some of the shows were based on Jewish folklore featuring Ida Kaminska and later, her daughter, Ruth."

The Family Business

"After the war, my mother and father started a private business, which ran contrary to the communist system they lived under. They were brave and going against the system. The business was lucrative but stressful. My mother ran the business alongside my father. My father was the doer, and she was the strategist, so she was more like the head of the operation.

"Employment was not easy for Jewish people in the Polish system. They did not know the language and faced discrimination. They did not have marketable skills. I believe that situation pushed my parents to develop their business acumen. Most people who were employed worked for a socialist enterprise. My parents took a risk by owning their own business.

"My mother and father ran the business from our home and employed a few people as well. We were more comfortable than many Polish families who lived paycheck to paycheck. I worked for my parents too, for extra cash." This private initiative was rare for the time and place. In communist Poland, the goal was income equality or wealth distribution, so private enterprise was frowned upon.

"When I graduated from Peretz and went to college, I became a lab technician. My monthly salary was $1500 zloty. That was really not much. Prices were high. To buy a television, you would have to save up for months. You couldn't afford many shoes. There were shortages in stores. No luxuries. All money went into food."

The I. L. Peretz School

"The Jewish school was not so much a religious school but a public school with the addition of Jewish literature and Jewish language. Our school was known as the I. L. Peretz School, named after a classical writer in the 19th century who was almost as well-known as Sholem Aleichem. Today, many students keep in touch from all over the world, and we call ourselves Peretzniks (that is the Yiddish version of plural).

"The building was fairly big, maybe two floors. Now that I think about it, more likely three. Most of the activity took place on the second floor. The first floor included the gym, something like a cafeteria, and some elementary classrooms. The second floor was the high school. If you started at grade one at age six or seven, you were in the same building for the next eleven years. We wore uniforms. You had to wear black or navy, and we each wore a garment over our clothes with a white collar (somewhat like a dickie). Looking back at school ID pictures, I can see we wore these.

"There was no kindergarten; we started at grade one. I was maybe six and a half years old when I started. I graduated from that school after finishing high school. It was a second home to me.

"I am not a very outgoing person, and I did not have any close relationships with our teachers. I felt a gulf with some of the teachers because they were much older. Also, some of them were Russians, and we experienced cultural/communication issues. There were some younger teachers who were Polish, and I could relate to them better. One teacher was very young actually. All of us were very fond of him because he would take us out on field trips and fun outings.

"Some teachers were widows and rather dour. Often, they were not very good at managing a rowdy classroom. This is nothing unusual. I am sure it is going on every day in every school. So the cause was not that these teachers were survivors. It was just something I observed at our school.

"The school director commanded a lot of respect. He also taught math. I believe most of the teachers were sympathetic to the socialist system. It was a public school, and they probably had to comply with the program and curriculum. There were a lot of things that were left out of the curriculum at that school. We did not know the Soviets invaded Poland in 1939. The Soviets were painted as our friends. And we were taught Russian—for me, not very successfully."

The school was a microcosm, making Monica's world appear safe. "Soon we were teenagers, and we had parties, not homecoming like in America but graduation parties. There was romance and teenage angst, but this was the small world I inhabited. We were very close because I graduated with only ten classmates. As you can imagine, we knew each other very well. Thank goodness for Facebook. Prior to the popularity of Facebook, we really lost touch. Several of my former classmates live in Sweden, some in Australia, others in the US and Israel. There was no way we could really keep in touch on a bigger scale. Thanks to Facebook, we can see each other's pictures and posts.

"When I was six or so, in first grade (1955, before the big Aliyah where numerous families left), many families had repatriated from Russia, and our class size grew quickly. They had survived the war in Russia and were coming home. They returned to Poland with their families and children after an agreement was made between Poland and Russia. I was overwhelmed with the swelling of our class size."

A Legacy of Warped History

Monica had noted that the history lessons they received at school were "sanitized in the sense that nothing bad about the Soviets could be said, and a lot of facts were just left out." She shared a story to illustrate the unfortunate legacy of such omissions.

"Up until recently—and I mean recently—maybe a few weeks ago [this is January 2022], I was not aware of the existence of the Łòdz Ghetto. I imagine there must be others kept in the dark like me. The reason I was unaware was because the Communist party kept things from us. As I said, they were not very open and honest about history. We didn't know what the Łòdz Ghetto was. I knew about other ghettos. My father was in the Warsaw Ghetto because he was from that area. The way I found out recently was from reading on the internet. On the internet you can find out everything. I read somewhere that there was a ghetto in Łòdz. I shudder to think of the number of times I walked through the area without knowing its history.

"If you travel to Europe, you see many cities with a market or a square at the epicenter. Łòdz is built a little bit differently because of its location," Monica explains. "There is this big square, Freedom Square, and in the middle stands a large monument honoring Tadeusz Kościuszko. (Kościuszko is a hero in both Poland and America; he went to fight for American freedom in the Revolutionary War.) From that big square several streets branch out. One is the main street, Piotrowska, and I lived just a few blocks from it (half a mile or so). It's a very long street, something like eight or ten kilometers.

"Łòdz is not famous for many things, but it is famous for the National Film School [The Łòdz Film School]," Monica comments. "The school trains aspiring movie makers. Many notable filmmakers, including cinematographer Pawel Edelman (The Pianist), and the infamous director Roman Polansky studied at this school. Actors and actresses were trained there as well. I mention this because when I was maybe eight or nine, walking home from school one day, I came upon a huge artificial brick wall in front of our building. It was part of a movie set. People were making a movie on my street! That brick wall was supposed to be a wall of the ghetto. I learned the movie had the name Samson in the title, and that's all I ever knew. The sheer size of that wall allowed only a small corridor to enter my house. This image stays in mind vividly. I don't know much more about what happened to the wall or the movie." The movie most likely was the Polish Samson released in 1961, and the wall actually represented the Warsaw Ghetto. But for Monica, the movie set planted an idea that there might have been a ghetto near her home.

Monica's Family

"My father survived the Warsaw Ghetto, Auschwitz, and Buchenwald during the war 1939-1945. But I don't like to call him a prisoner because that implies that he committed a crime. He didn't. During that time, it was the criminals that ran wild outside the cages in a frightening loss of reason.

But despite the years he spent imprisoned, he never lost his humanity and was a doting parent to my brother and me. My parents provided us with necessities quite well but were not in the habit of spoiling us with gifts. So one day when my father came back from a business trip to Warsaw bringing back a present—a little book—it stood out as something very special. The fact that it's still in my possession after so many years is a miracle in itself because I have almost nothing from my childhood in Poland.

"It is no secret about where my parents were during the war.

Monica's Little Book still survives today!

My father was in Auschwitz, and I have documents. I also grew up with him wearing his tattoo. I didn't understand what it meant as a child, but now I do. When we were leaving Poland, he needed documents, so I have a document that specifies the dates of his imprisonment—because we know the Germans documented everything. The number on the paper corresponds to the number tattooed on his forearm.

"As I mentioned, my mother and her sister were very close. At their father's insistence, they turned themselves in to the Germans, because they were young girls and perhaps had a chance to survive as laborers. There was a belief that if you were young and strong and if you turned yourself in, you would make it through the war in a labor camp (as opposed to a death camp). So, they went together, hoping for the best outcome.

"My mother and her sister survived the war, and they ended up back in Łòdz. They were liberated in Germany, and I believe traveled back to Poland mostly by foot, the reason being there were no trucks available. By then everything had been blown up. My mother had injured feet to prove that she had survived this long-distance walk. Despite the distance, they described the trip back as a happy occasion because they were going home. However, it was also a perilous journey and rife with danger. The Germans and the Soviets were shooting at each other in those areas, and these two women could have been caught in the crossfire. You could get killed on the way home after liberation just as easily as before the armistice. But both sisters survived and somehow got themselves to Łòdz.

"My father came to Łòdz as well, a city that didn't suffer much destruction during the war unlike Warsaw, for instance, which was bombed in 1939. Łòdz was somehow spared, so a lot of Jewish families landed in Łòdz ready to start a new life, including my family."

When Monica's family arrived in Łòdz, they needed to find a way to support themselves, to make a living. "Many of the Jewish families were going into businesses of their own. As you can imagine, after the war there was a shortage of everything, which included shoes, both for children and adults. My father went into partnership, a private business, with two brothers as shoemakers."

After the war, Jews were keeping to tradition and giving Jewish names. To avoid antisemitism and to keep us from being targets, unofficially we had Polish names. My Jewish name is Golda. If you follow Jewish tradition, you name the children after a close relative who is deceased. My mother wanted me to have his mother's name, which was Golda. My Polish name was Gienia, which later was changed to Monica.

"Because we lived in Poland, the Yiddish names did not resonate well in the workplace. My mother sometimes went by Felicia, which is a Polish version of her name." Fagja's name appears on some wartime documents as Fela, but Monica is not familiar with this version of her mother's name.

Antisemitism was almost part of society: it was us and it was them. Us—Jews, and them—the Goyim (non-Jews). It was unofficial; I guess Goyim would be offensive to them. We didn't speak it out loud, but this is how we felt. My mom's version of the Hebrew word us or we was anahno. Because the word was corrupted throughout the years, my mother would say, "Anhoo." When she would meet a person in the park or the street, and if she wanted to know if this person was Jewish, she would ask, "Anhoo?" It was code for "Are you one of us?"

"I am somewhat ambivalent about that. On one hand, yes, it was undeniable that Jews were separated from the Polish Christian society. But on the other hand, my parents made their living by having business with the Polish Christian society. Through this business, we met a lot of Poles who were friendly, lovely, and nice. They were also good customers. If you hear about a lot of antisemitism in Poland, it is true, but it is only one aspect of life in Poland. Yes, it was there, but there was also a segment of society that was friendly and helpful. And the Jewish people survived because of their kindness, piety, and good hearts (of some)."

Chapter Eleven
Leaving Łòdz

Monica describes her childhood as a largely carefree life. She explains, "The war was over. The '50s and the '60s were relatively peaceful and quiet until 1967. When Israel entered the Six-Day War, that's when things changed. Up to that point, there was not much upheaval in my life. (Other relatives, especially young boys, reported feeling unsafe as they were growing up.) After school, I spent time with my friends. I had the usual growing up problems and tribulations but nothing too dramatic.

"When I got a little older in my adolescence and teenage years, I enjoyed Polish literature, particularly by writers who thrived in the period between the two world wars when Poland briefly experienced independence. The plays, novels, and poems of that time all clicked with me. There are patriotic and romantic themes in those works.

"The relevance of my attraction to earlier time periods is that nothing happens in isolation. There is a connection with what happens in the past and what happens in the future. Poland is so central in Europe; there is always someone who wants part of it. Prussia, Russia, and Austria are the three empires that divided what we know as Poland among themselves in the 18th century. A 19th-century Romantic poet and writer named Adam Mickiewicz, who had believed in an independent Poland, wrote during that time of Polish partition epic poems and dramas about Poland being dominated by other nations. His works had a huge influence on generations of Polish writers." In late 1967, a play by Mickiewicz, Dzaidy (Forefathers' Eve), considered a classic of Polish literature, was banned by the Polish government. An outcry erupted and sparked a student revolt in March 1968. Unrest had been brewing for quite a while in postwar Poland. Another contributing factor to the uprising was the Polish regime's anti-

Zionist campaign, which had been launched following the Israeli victory in the 1967 Six Day War.

"The events of March 1968, caused many people, including my cousins, to leave Poland amidst the new wave of antisemitism. My parents had their business almost from 1949–1968 when the political climate was changing, and a lot of Jewish families were leaving. By then, my parents were ready for retirement. During the aftermath of March 1968, we had an opportunity to leave Poland and go to Denmark. Though we didn't leave right away, we did emigrate in 1971.

"My parents opted for Denmark because it was close and wasn't as intimidating as traveling to America or Israel. Denmark seemed the safest place to go, and it was offering political asylum because we were considered victims of political discrimination based on the Six Day War in Israel in 1967 and increase in antisemitism in Poland in 1968."

Monica is looking forward to meeting her new cousins, and enjoys regular conversations with her cousin, Sandi Solomon. "Meeting new family members (even virtually) is the icing on the family cake.

Epilogue
Sandi Torgovnick Solomon

How often does one get to meet family that one thought had died in the Holocaust seventy years ago?

I have always envied people with large families. Now, thanks to my new cousins, I have been blessed to have a large family, a family with wonderful people whom I communicate with often.

This project was written for my sons and their families. I wanted them to know about their cousins and the history of our family. Having family members who survived the Holocaust and a document describing their lives would make the Holocaust less abstract. While there are many Holocaust accounts out there, I thought our history was truly unique. We lost most of our family but found we could still make a connection with the very special ones we have found.

On March 20, 2021, Marvin and I had our first cousins visit. Almost a year later, we were treated to a visit with the Singer-Katz family. On March 19, 2022, Ari Solomon married Meera Nathan in Atlanta, Georgia. Ari is my son Eric's son and perhaps may start a new generation of Solomons. Helen Singer-Katz, together with her husband and son, Dan, attended the wedding. Also present was her brother, Geoffrey Bar-Lev.

This is significant because all my grandchildren were there to meet their cousins. To see Geoffrey dancing with his cousins and to dance with him myself is a miracle. This is the first time that I have been together with these two cousins. What was an interesting story about two brothers and their sisters has become a tale about my family.

Geoffrey lives near my son Eric in Atlanta. When Geoffrey visits, he frequently sees my granddaughter, Adina, and my grandson, Yonah, and sometimes his brother Ari. Eric's family has grown close to Geoffrey, a frequent house guest. Geoffrey has also become close with my brother, Stuart. The family is now growing together and starting to be supportive of each other.

I have been a longtime supporter of Israel. In fact, support of Israel has been a key part of my philosophy. Each of my cousins needed a safe political haven to escape the maltreatment in Europe. My children and grandchildren who live in a sheltered environment in the USA, do not understand this need for a haven. Documenting the lives of these new cousins should allow my family to relate to the significance of a Jewish homeland on a personal basis. Readers of this saga should also empathize with the cousins and understand the need for Israel.